"It is difficult to estimate the value of the freedom gained by anyone receiving this instruction. Our calling for stewardship of God's provision is clearly defined and Biblically directed. I recommend this book as *required reading* to all desiring to serve our Lord in personal life and public ministry."

—**Michael Millé,** *Pastor*
White Dove Fellowship Church
and International Outreach Center

"This is a practical, common sense handbook that every Christian should have. It gives a broad view of the financial landscape and how Christians can be effective in their use of money. The information in this book would cost a fortune if you had to get it from financial consultants and seminars. And there is a pervasive Christian perspective here, too. I heartily recommend Robert's *Money Came by the House the Other Day*."

—**Ronald E. Cottle, Ph.D., Ed.D.,** *President,*
Christian Life School of Theology, Columbus, GA

"To all my friends, I have one cry! Read and re-read this book! How I wish I could have had this material when we started our home ... and our church. It would have saved me many hours and days of distress. This is a "Financial and Business Book," but it is a deeply "Spiritual Book." Bob Katz takes the principles of the Word of God and applies them to every financial problem you could ever imagine. He takes complicated things and makes them easy.

If you are frustrated and in a financial 'house of mirrors,' Bob Katz shows you the 'way out' in his book. By reading this book and applying its principles, you will be blessed beyond your dreams ... and you will learn the rich reward of God's 'Money Secrets.'"

—**Charles Edward Green,** *Pastor*
Faith Church, New Orleans, LA

Money Came by the House the Other Day

A Guide to
Christian Financial Planning
and Stories of Stewardship

Money Came by the House the Other Day

A Guide to Christian Financial Planning and Stories of Stewardship

Robert W. Katz, CPA, MS

with Jamie Katz

InSync
PRESS

Published by InSync Communications LLC, InSync Press
2445 River Tree Circle
Sanford, FL 32771
http://www.insyncpress.com
407-688-1156

This book was set in Adobe Janson Text
Cover Design and Composition by Jonathan Pennell

Library of Congress Catalog Number: 2001087004
        Katz, Robert W.
Money Came by the House the Other Day
        ISBN: 1-929902-14-X

First InSync Press Edition
10   9   8   7   6   5   4   3   2
Printed in the United States of America

Dedication

I HAVE BEEN TRULY BLESSED IN MY LIFE by two men who have had a profound influence upon my spiritual growth. Pastor Charles Green of Faith Church is my father figure. For over twenty five years his love and support have been without boundary. And, Pastor Michael Millé of White Dove Fellowship is my fire figure. His passion and challenge to "ask for the nations" have set my spirit ablaze.

From the bottom of my heart I thank you both for being such dedicated men of God.

Acknowledgements

"A wife of noble character who can find ...
Her husband has full confidence in her ...
She brings him good not harm all the days of her life.
She sets about her work vigorously;
She speaks with wisdom and faithful instruction
in her tongue ...
Her children arise and call her blessed: her
husband also and he praises her ...
Charm is deceptive, and beauty is fleeting;
but a woman who fears the Lord is to be praised.
Give her the reward she has earned and
let her works bring her praise at the city gate."
(Proverbs 31:10,11,12,17,26,28,30,31)

One of the Lord's most precious gifts to me is my wife Jamie.

Her creative input and hours of rewriting and editing helped to breathe life, clarity and refinement onto these pages. Without her this would not be.

Thank you for your major contribution to this book and for your unending love and support.

*T*he Lord will send a blessing on
your barns and on everything
you put your hand to. The Lord your God
will bless you in the land he is giving you.
The Lord will establish you as his
holy people, as he promised you on
oath, if you keep the commands of
the Lord your God and walk in his
Ways. Then all the peoples on earth
will see that you are called by the
name of the Lord, and they will fear
you. The Lord will grant you abundant
prosperity — in the fruit of your
womb, the young of your livestock
and the crops of your ground — in the
land he swore to your forefathers to
give you.

The Lord will open the heavens,
the storehouse of his bounty, to
send rain on your land in season
and to bless all the work of your hands.
You will lend to many nations but will
borrow from none. The Lord will
make you the head, not the tail. If you
pay attention to the commands of the
Lord your God that I give you this day
and carefully follow them, you will always
be at the top, never at the bottom.
Do not turn aside from any of
the commands I give you today, to the
right or to the left, following other
gods and serving them.
(Deuteronomy 28:8-14)

About The Author

ROBERT W. KATZ has been a partner in a New Orleans-based certified public accounting firm for the last twenty-two years. His areas of specialty include personal financial planning, tax and estate planning, and health care consulting. He received a bachelor's degree from Louisiana State University and a master's degree from the University of New Orleans. He is a Certified Public Accountant and a Registered Investment Advisor. Bob is the author of *The Physician's Survival Guide to the Business of Medicine* and *The Family Practitioner's Survival Guide to the Practice of Medicine*.

This book was born of his deep desire to serve the Lord by offering Bible-based wisdom on topics that virtually everyone struggles with throughout their lives — financial planning and stewardship. Bob is a frequent speaker at churches and at national and international medical conferences.

He resides in New Orleans with his wife and co-author, Jamie, and their two children.

JAMIE KATZ is a native of New Orleans. She earned a Bachelor of Arts degree from Loyola University where she majored in communications. She is presently an active member of her church, White

Dove Fellowship. In addition to writing with her husband, she enjoys intercession and teaching a Bible-based Leaders Acquiring Freedom class. Jamie and her husband Bob have been married for 19 years.

Contents

Testimonials

Dedication vii

Acknowledgements ix

About The Author ix

Foreword *by Oral Roberts* xvii

PART I — "THE CONDITION OF YOUR FLOCKS"

1. **Money Talks** 1

2. **Financial Straight Talk**
   "But what about you ...Who do you say I am?" 5

3. **Sink Hole**
   Devoted to Debt 15

4. **The Condition of Your Flocks — I**
   Preparing Your Personal Balance Sheet 19

5. **Ice Cream**
   How Much Is Enough? 31

6. **The Condition of Your Flocks — II**
   Preparing Your Personal Income Statement 37

7. **Monopoly**
   The Remains of the Day 45

8. **Confessions of a Balance Sheet**
   Wise Analysis Breaks Financial Paralysis 47

9. **Scrooge**
   Turned Off to Tithing 57

10. **Income Statement Analysis**
   God, Caesar and You 63

PART II — "GIVE PORTIONS TO SEVEN, YES EIGHT

11. **Before We Begin**
   A Word or Two on Investing 77

12. **Monopolife**
   Your Time or Your Money? 85

13. **Cash**
   The Emergency Fund 93

14. **Stocks**
   Eggs in a Basket 103

15. **Bonds**
   Steady and Sure? 117

16. **Gimme Shelter**
   How to Buy a House 131

17. **Ralph**
   Insurance for Eternity 147

18. **Risky Business**
    How to Buy Various Types of Insurance 153

19. **School Days**
    The High Cost of Higher Education 171

20. **The Gold Watch**
    Planning for Retirement 179

21. **Reader's Choice**
    The Eighth Portion 197

22. **Your Inheritance**
    The Living Bible 201

Epilogue 209

Foreword

MANY YEARS AGO, THE MOTHER of a little Jewish boy was a strong believer in God and His miracle power.

One day when her little son, Robert, was seriously ill, she placed his hand on the television set as I stretched out my hands to pray a healing prayer for the sick. Robert was healed and we were contacted.

Robert grew up and in his early twenties accepted Jesus as his personal Savior and Lord. Later he became a Certified Public Accountant with the belief that the Lord is the only One who knows all about money. So his study was double: learning how to become a Certified Public Accountant and combining it with the Word of God which he studied with equal time.

To his amazement he discovered all money is Bible based and its use, when directed by the Lord, brings happiness and lasting accomplishment. With His guidance, financial success is not only attainable, but brings two things indispensable to our present and eternal welfare: constant gain and lasting contentment of mind and heart.

Robert Katz has been the CPA for some of my closest personal friends, including many successful pastors. His skillful and anointed weaving of the getting of money and the biblical use of it is enhanced by a wonderful way of writing stories from God's Word and his experiences with people just like you and me.

I wish I had had this book when I began my healing ministry 53 years ago as a young, unknown preacher with little money and even less knowledge of how to fulfill Paul's statement:

"The workman is worthy of his his hire."
(I Timothy 5:18)

I also wish that when my ministry began meeting the needs of great numbers of people, and I had to make proper use of the income for expenses and continual expansion of my ministry, that I could have had a book like Robert Katz has finally written. Only God knows how much better I would have handled those financial affairs, as well as provided for my wife Evelyn and myself for our golden years.

Humbly, but enthusiastically, I urge you: READ THIS BOOK, STUDY IT, AND CHECK THE SCRIPTURES USED ALONGSIDE THE CPA FACTS. I say you will advance your finances with skill and integrity and also your life with lasting peace and contentment.

— **Oral Roberts**
Founder / Chancellor
Oral Roberts University
Tulsa, Oklahoma

PART

I

The Condition of Your Flocks

1

Money Talks

MONEY CAME BY THE HOUSE the other day. As soon as I opened the door to let him in I sensed that something was wrong. He walked aimlessly into the living room and plopped himself into my favorite chair.

"Okay, if I sit here?"

"Sure, Money, can I get you something to drink?" Money sometimes drops by to discuss his problems, so I wasn't totally surprised to see him looking so discouraged.

"Got any diet drinks?" He waited to catch my eye and then added, "I've put on a few pounds lately." I just shook my head. Money was the master of the bad pun.

I handed him his drink and then we got down to business.

"Money, if you don't mind me saying so you look horrible. You haven't been fighting with Greed again have you?"

"No, it's just that I'm depressed." He looked at me with those sad green eyes and continued on.

"I get blamed for everything. Everything! A man gets himself deep into debt. Does he face up to his problem? No, he whines, 'I just don't have enough Money.' A woman gets into a terrible fight with her husband. Do they try to understand what they are really fighting over? No, it's always, 'We are fighting over Money.' I'm hoarded, I'm stolen, I'm wasted and I'm misunderstood.

"Just yesterday, I was walking down the street and someone stopped me and said, 'Aren't you Security?' Before I could answer they blurted out, 'No, no, you're not Security, you're Glamour. No? Well, you sure look like Glamour to me.'"

Money looked over at me and I thought he was going to burst into tears. "You know I am not God," his sad voice trailed off and he sank back into my easy chair.

Just then my wife walked into the living room, "Hey, honey, look — it's Money."

My sweet wife, Jamie, unaware of what was being discussed, blurted out, "Money, are you feeling okay? You don't look well." And he was off again.

"I'm fine, I'm fine, it's people that make me crazy!"

Jamie looked over at me and I just rolled my eyes and motioned for her to sit down.

"I'm a complex creation. Did you know that there are over two thousand verses in the Bible that talk about me? Did you know that over half the parables mention me?"

Before we could say anything Money answered his own questions. "No, of course not.

"God writes a book that completely explains me, but does anyone take the time to read it? No, they just grab at me, and pull on me and throw me around like dogs fighting over an old bone.

"Nobody treats Charity like that. Everyone loves Charity, but if it wasn't for me Charity would be a nobody."

Jamie and I just listened. Sometimes when Money was having troubles the best thing to do was just be attentive.

"Do the two of you remember Solomon? I gave that boy every-thing. But, he respected me. I can remember like it was yesterday that time we had lunch and he told me, 'You know, Money,

> *"Whoever loves money never has*
> *money enough;*
> *whoever loves wealth is never*
> *satisfied with his income."*
> **(Ecclesiastes 5:10)**

"Now that was a smart kid who really understood me. He appreci-ated my finer qualities."

Money eased back into my chair and for the first time that day I saw him smile. Thinking about the good old days with Solomon appeared to have a calming effect.

"Jamie, Bob — you know what I am?"

Jamie and I looked at each other not quite sure how to respond.

"Well, I'll tell you. In the end I am simply a magnifying glass for a man's heart. I really never give or take, I just magnify what is already in a man's heart. People with anger in their hearts become angrier and use me to dominate others. People with fear in their hearts use me to build a bigger fortress to hide behind. Lust with Money turns into addictions of every kind. And with enough Money and Pride you become your own god.

"On the other hand, a content heart uses Money for great service. Hope with Money gives birth to actions of help and comfort. Humility and Money fills the world with secret acts of kindness. And a heart full of love uses me to create more love, like ripples on a pond."

Money got up and walked to my front door.

"Money, you feeling better?"

"Yeah, I guess it's not such a bad job after all. It just gets to me every once in a while."

"I understand."

We hugged and as he walked out the door he turned, gave me a little smile and said, "I guess I was just feeling a little spent."

2

Financial Straight Talk

"But what about you ... Who do you say I am?"
(Matthew 16:15)

THE ECONOMIC ENGINE of the most powerful country in the world jets forward as if on automatic pilot. In its wake the stock market is climbing to new highs and unemployment is falling to new lows.

Everything is great, right?

Maybe.

Why does a closer look reveal consumer debt at an all time high? Why are more Americans declaring personal bankruptcy than ever before? And why do so many people feel that they are one pay check away from poverty and that their personal finances are spinning hopelessly out of control?

In order to understand the answers to these questions or discuss any aspect of personal financial planning, three foundational truths about your financial situation must be accepted.

TRUTH #1

THE BATTLE FOR YOUR FINANCES IS SPIRITUAL

The Bible clearly warns us that someone wants to destroy you:

> *"The thief comes only to steal and kill and destroy ..."*
> *(John 10:10)*

What better way to do it than through your finances? Spirits of lack, poverty, and greed roam the earth pitting husband against wife, parents against children and friend against friend. Our civil courts are clogged like dirty sewers with plaintiffs and defendants suing one another and demanding money as recompense. As a result marriages fail, relationships crumble, dreams are shattered and lives are destroyed.

But the good news is Someone greater wants to save you. The Bible tells us that our heavenly Father wants to bless you, literally that He wants to prepare a feast for you in the presence of your enemies — the very enemies that would try to destroy you (***Psalms 23:5***). A seat at His banquet table has one simple requirement:

> *"Delight yourself in the Lord and he will give you*
> *the desires of your heart."*
> *(Psalms 37:4)*

God has a plan for your life and it includes your economic well being. To deny this fact, to try and separate God from your finances is foolishness. There are over two thousand verses in the Bible about money and it is with good reason. The Lord knows that we will all face financial battles. He also knows that they are really spiritual in nature, and He wants to arm us with the best "instruction manual" ever written on financial planning. The Bible.

And so the beginning of financial wisdom is to understand that the battle is spiritual.

> *"For our struggle is not against flesh and blood,*
> *but against the rulers, against the authorities,*
> *against the powers of this dark world and*
> *against the spiritual forces of evil in the*
> *heavenly realms."*
> **(Ephesians 6:12)**

TRUTH #2

VICTORY COMES THROUGH SURRENDER

It's not ours. It's His.

> *"I am God, your God ...*
> *I have no need of a bull from your stall*
> *or goats from your pens,*
> *for every animal of the forest is mine,*
> *and the cattle on a thousand hills.*
> *I know every bird in the mountains,*
> *and the creatures of the field are mine.*
> *If I were hungry I would not tell you,*
> *for the world is mine, and all that is in it."*
> **(Psalms 50:7, 9-12)**

It's *all* His.

When we grasp this revelation, the next step is *surrender*. We must surrender ownership of our possessions, surrender the illusion that we are in control and surrender our wills to the reality that ... it's all His. Surrender first involves repentance for past financial sins. Scriptural repentance refers simply to a changing of direction from our way to God's way. Once we have repented we can then begin the process of renewing our minds through God's word to become better stewards over all that He has temporarily entrusted to us.

And that's a key point, our role is only that of temporary stewards. As **1 Timothy 6:7** explains,

> *"For we brought nothing into the world,*
> *and we can take nothing out of it."*
> **(1 Timothy 6:7)**

So what is the point? Why the constant financial struggles? Why all the Bible verses about money? Why all the parables about stewardship?

The point is beyond what many of us might ever imagine. *God uses our finances to develop our character.* Jesus uses parables regarding financial stewardship to teach us about the importance of developing Godly qualities such as perseverance, discipline, charity, compassion, sacrifice, integrity and honesty. Money is an ideal training tool because God knows

> *"... where your treasure is, there your heart will be also."*
> **(Matthew 6:21)**

And so, for the Christian, the goal of stewardship is much greater than simply paying your monthly bills. The goal is *preparation for eternity.*

> *"But you, man of God, flee from all this, and pursue righteousness, godliness, faith, love, endurance and gentleness.*
> *Fight the good fight of faith.*
> *Take hold of the eternal life to which you were called when you*

made your good confession in the presence of many witnesses."
(1 Timothy 6:11-12)

"In this way, they will lay up treasure for themselves as a firm foundation for the coming age so that they may take hold of the life that is truly life."
(1 Timothy 6:19)

By teaching us financial stewardship the Lord is preparing us for the day of eternal accounting where we will discover that,

"Whoever can be trusted with very little can also be trusted with much, and whoever is dishonest with very little will also be dishonest with much.
So if you have not been trustworthy in handling worldly wealth, who will trust you with true riches?
And if you have not been trustworthy with someone else's property, who will give you property of your own?"
(Luke 16:10-12)

The eternal stakes are so high that it becomes our duty to learn all that we can about stewardship, which brings us to the last fundamental truth.

TRUTH # 3

YOU MUST SEEK OUT FINANCIAL WISDOM

"... my people are destroyed from lack of knowledge."
(Hosea 4:6)

No one was born with financial wisdom ... and few are taught it. Yet, every day we are faced with countless financial decisions that we are unprepared to deal with. We can't steward what we don't understand and this lack of knowledge creates a spiritual vacuum. A spiritual vacuum will never remain empty — one of two things will happen.

It will be filled by a proper relationship with the Lord, or Satan will continually entice us to fill it with counterfeits.

For example, the enemy uses the world system to try and deceive us with the lie of the self-made man. Many falsely believe that we are in control and that the answer is found in more money, more lifestyle and more power. The message ingrained in us from childhood is to seek success, not a savior. Satan whispers to us, "You don't need the Lord, you need a Lexus."

It's a lie.

> *"Command those who are rich in this present world not to be arrogant nor to put their hope in wealth, which is so uncertain, but to put their hope in God, who richly provides us with everything for our enjoyment. Command them to do good, to be rich in good deeds, and to be generous and willing to share."*
> **(1 Timothy 6:17-18)**

There are others whom Satan tempts with the illusion of the easy way, the big hit, the home run ... the winning lottery ticket, the right stock or even a law suit that will make them rich. It seems harmless, but —

It's a lie.

> *"People who want to get rich fall into temptation and a trap and into many foolish and harmful desires that plunge men into ruin and destruction. For the love of money is a root of all kinds of evil. Some people, eager for money, have wandered from the faith and pierced themselves with many griefs."*
> **(1 Timothy 6:9-10)**

Jesus knew the truth. That is why over half of the parables in the Bible deal with economic matters. Don't be confused by the fact that He spoke in terms of grapes and wine, bread and oil, sheep and cattle ... that was the medium of exchange, the money of His day. He spoke in terms very real to the people of that time and His message then, as now, is very simple ... *seek wisdom.*

> *"The fear of the Lord is the beginning of knowledge, but fools despise wisdom and discipline."*
> **(Proverbs 1:7)**

We must

> *"... remember the Lord your God, for it is he who gives you the ability to produce wealth, ..."*
> **(Deuteronomy 8:18)**

We must search the scriptures to hear His loving instruction:

> *"My son do not forget my teaching but keep my commands in your heart, for they will prolong your life many years and bring you prosperity."*
> **(Proverbs 3:1)**

And then we will be transformed into wise stewards:

> *"Blessed is the man who finds wisdom, the man who gains understanding, for she is more profitable than silver and yields better returns than gold. She is more precious than rubies; nothing you desire can compare with her. Long life is in her right hand; in her left hand are riches and honor."*
> **(Proverbs 3:13-17)**

In over twenty-five years of counseling people about financial matters I have never experienced a problem whose answer could not be found in scripture. The goal of this book is to help you gain insight into some of the Biblical financial wisdom that the Lord has prepared for all of us.

This book is divided into two parts, each based on a foundational scripture.

Part I is based on **Proverbs 27:23-24,**

> *"Be sure you know the condition of your flocks, give careful attention to your herds; for riches do not endure forever, and a crown is not secure for all generations."*

The first ten chapters will help you to "know the conditions of your flocks" by teaching you to organize, analyze and set goals for your personal finances.

Part II is based on **Ecclesiastes 11:1-2,**

> *"Cast your bread upon the waters, for after many days you will find it again. Give portions to seven, yes to eight, for you do not know what disaster may come upon the land."*

Part II will help you to become better stewards in eight important areas of your personal finances. We will study what the Bible has to say about cash, stocks, bonds, debt, your home, your insurances, educating your children, and preparing for retirement.

Our goal on earth is to claim the promise of **Ecclesiastes 5:19,**

> *"... when God gives any man wealth and possessions, and enables him to enjoy them, to accept his lot and be happy in his work —this is a gift from God. He seldom reflects on the days of his life because God keeps him occupied with gladness of heart."*

And our goal in heaven will be to hear his voice calling out to us,

"Well done, good and faithful servant!
You have been faithful with a few things;
I will put you in charge of many things.
Come and share your master's happiness!"
(Matthew 25:21)

3

Sink Hole

Devoted to Debt

MARK MATHEWS WAS GOING to have a bad day. It all started at breakfast when he walked over to the window to look at his new truck. What he saw made him spill hot coffee all over himself. His beautiful new Arizona Sky Blue pick-up truck was gone. Scalded, barefoot and still in his pajamas he bolted out of his front door only to discover that not only was his truck gone, but the driveway holding it and half of his front lawn were gone as well.

And just when he thought that it couldn't get any worse, it did. For the next twenty-four hours, Mr. Mathews watched helplessly as a sink hole steadily expanded until his entire house collapsed into the cavern.

It didn't take the insurance investigators very long to figure out what had happened. Mr. Mathews had built his house on what he had thought was a solid rock foundation. What he didn't know was that the rock was limestone and that there was a tiny trickle of water flowing underground.

Although I had no idea, I am told that any average high school chemistry student knows that one of water's many properties is that it can absorb carbon dioxide. And, it only takes a tiny amount of carbon dioxide to transform ordinary water into carbonic acid. Carbonic acid easily dissolves limestone. The more limestone the acid dissolves, the faster the water flows. The faster the water flows, the more limestone it dissolves until you have, as Mr. Mathews can attest to, a ravenous sink hole.

I was sitting at my desk reading the newspaper article about Mr. Mathew's dilemma when my next appointment arrived — a middle aged couple who had just become clients of our firm.

I wasn't sure why they had scheduled the appointment but from the looks on their faces I could tell that the reason wasn't a good one.

They began to tell me a story which, sadly, I hear too often.

The couple was approaching a time in their lives when they thought they would be able to slow down a little. The problem was that they had saved practically nothing. The husband's salary had all gone to maintaining a comfortable lifestyle, and when there had been trouble maintaining that lifestyle, they borrowed. And they borrowed and borrowed until their debts were staggering.

One by one they pulled official looking papers out of a leather briefcase and handed them to me. I laid them out across my desk knowing that they would end up being the pieces to an ugly puzzle.

Their house had two mortgages on it, there were four car notes, and twelve credit cards had almost forty thousand dollars of debt charged on them. There was a bank "consolidation" loan that lingered from the last time they had tried to clean up their financial mess and a past due credit union loan that they had taken out for their last family vacation.

The husband just sat there looking at my desk and shaking his head in disbelief. His wife's eyes filled with tears as she told me that their three children were rapidly approaching college age. The overwhelming reality of tuition, books, housing and living expenses was beginning to sink in. It was all becoming too clear: no early retirement, no slowing down, a questionable ability to retire at age sixty-five and perhaps bankruptcy.

Their debts had been harmless at first like a small trickle of water. They had purchased their house and car on time. Not bad decisions, as there is a valuable asset associated with the debt and very few of us can afford to buy either outright.

But, then the trickle began to flow a little faster, "Wouldn't it be nice to have ... why shouldn't we have ... it's only so much a month ..."

The distinction between wants and needs started to blur. Endless offers of easy credit flooded their mail box forming a steady stream of loans that began to erode the foundation of their finances.

Then came the fights over money, the desperation loans and the preposterous schemes.

And now a raging torrent of debt was pulling the whole family into a sink hole of financial ruin.

There they sat, afraid and confused, wondering what was to become of their lives.

Not all that much has changed in two thousand years. In **Matthew 6:25,** Jesus is teaching a large crowd about storing up treasures in heaven. He is patiently trying to explain to them that:

"... where your treasure is there your heart will be also."

Jesus is compassionate but unrelenting in his message,

"Therefore I tell you, do not worry about your life, what you will eat or drink; or about your body, what you will wear. But seek first his kingdom and his righteousness, and all these things will be given to you as well."

But how can we? With the burdens of this world so overwhelming, why is it so important that we look first to the kingdom of heaven?

Jesus' answer is simple,

"You cannot serve both God and Money."

His insight is profound,

"Either he will hate the one and love the other, or he will be devoted to the one and despise the other."

Jesus knows that our relationship with the Lord is shaped by what we think about throughout each day. If our thoughts primarily deal with money and worry over debt, our focus will separate us from our loving father.

Just as sure as a trickle of water can separate a well-built house from its foundation, a flood of financial worry will separate man from God. Therein lies the real loss ... both in this life and the next.

4

The Condition
of Your Flocks — I

Preparing Your Personal
Balance Sheet

"Suppose one of you wants to build a tower.
Will he not first sit down and estimate the cost to see
if he has enough money to complete it?
For if he lays the foundation and is not able to finish it,
everyone who sees it will ridicule him, saying,
'This fellow began to build and was not able to finish.'"
(Luke 14:28-30)

A YOUNG COUPLE CAME to my office recently. They were typical of many of the people that I consult with. He was a young doctor who had been in practice for about five years. His practice was doing very well and he was earning more money than he had ever dreamed of as a struggling resident. His wife was a nurse who had quit her job at a hospital to work full time in her husband's medical practice as the office manager.

The question they asked me is the one I hear over and over again from people of every income level, "Why can't we seem to get ahead?"

They went on to tell me, "We earn a good living, we're smart people ... but we just can't seem to figure out where all our money goes."

I began our meeting by asking them a few questions.

"Do you have regular financial statements prepared for your personal financial situation and for your medical practice?"

"Well, no, not really."

"Do you have a family budget?"

"No."

"Have you written down any financial goals?"

"Well, we'd like to have some money put away for our kids college expenses and for our retirement."

"Have you saved any money?"

"Not really, but our kids are young and we're a long way from retirement and ..."

Their financial plan is the equivalent of buying an expensive boat, setting it adrift in the ocean and hoping that it will float over to Europe where they will have a nice vacation. The truth is that when the storms come, and they will come, that boat may very likely meet with great peril.

I use the example of the physician to make a point. Here is a very smart man whom I know to be an excellent physician. If I were to go to him as a patient complaining of severe abdominal pain the first thing he would do is develop a detailed and written course of action. First, he would take down my medical history and then he would give me a complete physical examination. This would be followed by appropriate laboratory tests and any other diagnostic procedures that he felt would provide him with vital information about my condition. Once he had gathered and analyzed all of the pertinent data on my condition he would develop a diagnosis and execute a treatment plan with great precision.

But for his own financial health he has no data, no plan, and no course of action. He is a financial sieve with money coming in one end and flowing rapidly out of the other. It's the financial equivalent of malpractice and the Lord warns us against such ignorance,

> *"But everyone who hears these words of mine*
> *and does not put them into practice is like a*
> *foolish man who built his house on sand.*
> *The rain came down, the streams rose, and*
> *the winds blew and beat against that house,*
> *and it fell with a great crash."*
> ***(Matthew 7:26-27)***

God doesn't call us to be financial drifters whose financial planning consists merely of balancing our checkbook at the end of the month. This is the equivalent of building our financial homes on sand and will have a detrimental effect on our stewardship and spiritual maturity.

The Lord wants our financial homes built on solid rock. And laying this foundation is a two-step process:

STEP 1. YOU MUST CLEARLY **ORGANIZE** YOUR FINANCIAL SITUATION

STEP 2. YOU MUST REGULARLY **ANALYZE** YOUR FINANCIAL SITUATION AND MAKE NECESSARY ADJUSTMENTS

Chapters 4, 5 and 6 will help you clearly **organize** your personal financial situation. In this chapter you will learn how to prepare a simple *Balance Sheet* which reflects your family's current financial situation. Later, in Chapter 6 you will learn how to prepare an *Income Statement* which summarizes your family's income and expense activity. These two financial statements, the *Balance Sheet* and the *Income Statement*, will provide all the financial information you need to properly manage your personal finances.

Chapters 7, 8 and 9 will teach you how to **analyze** your financial situation and how to develop sound financial goals based on the information revealed by these two financial statements. So let's begin.

In order to help you prepare your own *Balance Sheet* and *Income Statement* we will use the Smith family as a fictional example.

THE SMITH FAMILY

Mr. Smith is an electrician who earns $35,000 a year and Mrs. Smith is a teacher earning $24,000 a year. They have $1,000 in their checking account and $3,500 deposited in a bank savings account. They also have $5,000 invested in stock mutual funds. The Smiths have a two-year-old family car and a sports utility vehicle. The total value of their automobiles is $27,000. They also have a boat worth $25,000. Their home is worth $170,000. They have cash surrender value in a life insurance policy on Mr. Smith's life of $2,500. Mr. Smith has a 401(k) plan were he works and the balance in his account is $15,000. Mrs. Smith's employer provides her with a pension plan in which she has $7,200. Their remaining assets consist of the furniture, fixtures and personal effects in their home which are all worth about $25,000.

In addition to what they **own**, the Smiths also **owe**.

They owe $130,000 on their first mortgage and they have a $25,000 second mortgage which they borrowed in order to buy their boat. They have a finance company loan of $8,600 that they used to buy some furniture and to pay some medical bills when their first child was born. They owe credit card companies $9,600. They owe $35,000 on auto loans and they still owe their parents $2,000 that they borrowed when they first got married.

So, what is the condition of the Smith's "flocks"?

You probably can't tell from just reading the information above. In order to really know we have to organize the Smith's personal financial situation into two basic financial statements. The first financial statement is the *Balance Sheet* and the second is the *Income Statement*.

THE BALANCE SHEET

The *Balance Sheet* is a listing of everything you own and everything you owe at one particular point in time.

Think of the *Balance Sheet* as someone snapping a picture of your personal financial situation and freezing everything at one moment in time. Everything in the picture that you own we will call your ASSETS and all of your debts we will refer to as your LIABILITIES.

It is important to see this correlation:

*Your **Balance Sheet** =*
Your Assets and Liabilities at One Point in Time

By subtracting all of your Liabilities from all of your Assets we obtain your NET WORTH at a particular point in time. A quick look at **Illustration 1** will help you to understand the simple structure of a *Balance Sheet.*

The point in time when most *Balance Sheets* occur is usually as of the end of a month, the end of a quarter or the end of a year. I suggest that you prepare your *Balance Sheet* as of the end of the most recent month and then update it at the end of every June and December.

We begin to prepare the Smith's *Balance Sheet* by listing all of their assets according to their *Liquidity. Liquidity* deals with the ease with which an asset can be converted into cash.

The most Liquid assets are called *CURRENT ASSETS. Current Assets* generally are cash or assets easily converted into cash. *Current Assets* also usually have the characteristic that their value is easy to establish. Savings, checking accounts, publicly traded stocks and bonds are all examples of *Current Assets.*

THE SMITH FAMILY
BALANCE SHEET
DECEMBER 31, 20XX

ASSETS		LIABILITIES & NET WORTH	
CURRENT ASSETS		**CURRENT LIABILITIES**	
CASH	$1,000	CREDIT CARD DEBT	$9,600
BANK SAVINGS ACCOUNT	3,500	FINANCE COMPANY LOAN	8,600
STOCK MUTUAL FUNDS	5,000		
TOTAL CURRENT ASSETS	**9,500**	**TOTAL CURRENT LIABILITIES**	**18,200**
FIXED ASSETS		**LONG-TERM DEBTS**	
RESIDENCE	170,000	FIRST MORTGAGE	130,000
AUTOMOBILES	27,000	SECOND MORTGAGE	25,000
FURNITURE, FIXTURES	25,000	AUTO LOANS	35,000
& PERSONAL EFFECTS		LOAN FROM PARENTS	2,000
BOAT	25,000		
TOTAL FIXED ASSETS	**247,000**	**TOTAL LONG-TERM DEBTS**	**192,000**
OTHER ASSETS		**TOTAL LIABILITIES**	**210,200**
LIFE INSURANCE CASH	2,500		
SURRENDER VALUE			
401 (K) PLAN	15,000		
PENSION PLAN	7,200		
TOTAL OTHER ASSETS	**24,700**	**NET WORTH**	**71,000**
TOTAL ASSETS	**$281,200**	**TOTAL LIABILITIES & NET**	**$281,200**

ILLUSTRATION 1

Looking at the *Current Asset* section of the Smith Family *Balance Sheet* we see that the Smiths have *Current Assets* which total $9,500. This consists of $1,000 of cash, $3,500 in their savings account and $5,000 that they have in the stock market.

Following *Current Assets* we list the less liquid assets which we will call *FIXED ASSETS*. Houses, automobiles, furniture, fixtures and personal goods are all examples of *Fixed Assets*.

Fixed Assets generally have two characteristics associated with them. First, it takes longer to convert a *Fixed Asset* into cash than a current asset. Second, it is usually harder to establish the exact value of a *Fixed Asset*. For example the money in the Smith's savings account has a readily identifiable value, $3,500. But, the value of their automobiles depends on many factors such as age, make, model, condition and the used car market when they try to sell it.

The last asset category is *OTHER ASSETS*. *Other Assets* are usually those assets that are easy to value but cannot be readily liquidated, usually due to a tax or legal restriction. Examples of *Other Assets* are IRA accounts, 401(k) accounts, annuities, life insurance values and pension accounts.

As you begin to list the assets on your own *Balance Sheet* remember these two rules:

1. Always list assets from the most liquid to the least liquid.
2. Always value non-cash assets at their *FAIR MARKET VALUE*

Fair Market Value is the value of an asset if it were to be sold on the open market between a willing seller and a willing buyer. In some cases the asset may have appreciated in value since you purchased it. For example if you have owned your home for several years it is probably worth more now than what your originally paid for it. List it at its current value on your *Balance Sheet*.

On the other hand, assets such as your furniture, fixtures, personal effects and automobiles will probably be worth much less than you paid for them — these assets have depreciated in value. List them at their reduced value on your Balance Sheet.

Look at **Illustration 1**, the Smith Family *Balance Sheet*.

The Smiths looked at the want ads in their local newspaper and valued their automobiles at $27,000. Their boat was similarly valued at $25,000. They know from comparable housing sales in their neighborhood that if they were to sell their home it would probably net them $170,000 after the expenses of the sale. The Smiths estimate that if they were forced to sell their furniture, fixtures, household goods, personal effects, jewelry, etc. they would net approximately $25,000. When valuing non-cash assets the best approximation of *Fair Market Value* is often an educated guess. Guess low.

Finally, the Smiths have placed three of their assets into the *Other Assets* category: the cash surrender value of their life insurance at $2,500, their 401(k) plan valued at $15,000 and their pension plan valued at $7,200.

The Smiths have now completed their list of everything they own as of one particular point in time and the total is $281,200. Sounds impressive, but is it?

Well, we can't tell for sure until we complete the *Balance Sheet* by listing everything that the Smiths owe.

Liabilities should be listed in the same manner as assets. Those liabilities that should be paid off within 12 to 24 months we will call *CURRENT LIABILITIES*. The liabilities that will take more than two years to pay off we will call *LONG-TERM DEBTS OR LONG-TERM LIABILITIES*.

The Smith's *Current Liabilities* consist of the $9,600 they owe to credit card companies and the $8,600 that they owe to a finance company.

Their *Long-Term Debts* consist of a $130,000 first mortgage, a $25,000 second mortgage, automobile notes that total $35,000 and the $2,000 that they owe their parents.

All of the Smith's liabilities total $210,200 and therefore their *Net Worth* at this particular point in time is $71,000.

Now that the Smiths have an accurate picture of their *Net Worth* we can state one of the basic goals of financial stewardship:

GOOD FINANCIAL STEWARDSHIP GENERALLY INVOLVES OVERSEEING ASSETS AND LIABILITIES IN A MANNER WHICH INCREASES NET WORTH

So how is that done?

In most cases all increases to *Net Worth* will come through proper management of the other key financial statement, *THE INCOME STATEMENT*.

I generally hate to use sports analogies, however, it seems appropriate to use one now.

The *Balance Sheet* and the *Income Statement* together can be compared to a football game. The *Balance Sheet* is the scoreboard. At any point in time during a football game you can know how the game is going if you look at the scoreboard. Likewise, at any point in time you can know the state of your finances if you look at your *Balance Sheet*.

YOUR FAMILY
BALANCE SHEET
DECEMBER 31, 20XX

ASSETS

CURRENT ASSETS

CASH
BANK SAVINGS ACCOUNT
STOCK MUTUAL FUNDS

TOTAL CURRENT ASSETS

FIXED ASSETS

RESIDENCE
AUTOMOBILES
FURNITURE, FIXTURES
    & PERSONAL EFFECTS
BOAT

TOTAL FIXED ASSETS

OTHER ASSETS

LIFE INSURANCE CASH
    SURRENDER VALUE
401 (K) PLAN
PENSION PLAN

TOTAL OTHER ASSETS

TOTAL ASSETS

LIABILITIES & NET WORTH

CURRENT LIABILITIES

CREDIT CARD DEBT
FINANCE COMPANY LOAN

TOTAL CURRENT LIABILITIES

LONG-TERM DEBTS

FIRST MORTGAGE
SECOND MORTGAGE
AUTO LOANS
LOAN FROM PARENTS

TOTAL LONG-TERM DEBTS

TOTAL LIABILITIES

NET WORTH

TOTAL LIABILITIES & NET

ILLUSTRATION 2

And just as a football scoreboard is changed by the activity on the playing field, your *Balance Sheet* will be changed by the activity reflected on your *Income Statement*.

This interrelationship between the *Balance Sheet* and the *Income Statement* is an important concept that we will discuss often in the following chapters. You must come to understand that all of your financial actions, your earning and spending decisions, directly impact your *Balance Sheet*. And it is your *Balance Sheet* that defines the "state of your flocks."

As we will see in Chapter 6, by taking dominion over your *Income Statement* and following the Lord's plan for your finances you can create a storm-proof *Balance Sheet*.

Chapter 6 will teach you how to prepare an *Income Statement*. But, first use **Illustration 2** to carefully construct your own personal *Balance Sheet*.

5

Ice Cream

How Much is Enough?

MY THREE-YEAR-OLD SON is at that age where he wants to do everything for himself. His motto has become, "I do dat."

Last week he asked me if he could have some ice cream for a snack. Sure, it was four o'clock in the afternoon and dinner was in an hour, but mom wasn't home, so I pulled out the ice cream scooper ... and two spoons and two bowls.

"I do dat." Jonathan wanted to scoop the ice cream into his bowl.

"You think you can scoop the ice cream into your bowl all by yourself?"

"Yeah." He gave me that "no problem" look so I handed it all over to him.

Jonathan sat down on the floor and dug in. He scooped and he scooped until a small mountain of ice cream began to rise above the ridge of his bowl. Every once in a while he'd look up from his excavation work, give me big smile, and then bore into the carton again. He was on a mission to put as much ice cream into that bowl as he could.

"So, Jonathan, how much ice cream can you eat?"

"I don't know." Scoop, scoop ... scoop.

"Well, do you think you have enough there?"

"No." Scoop, scoop ... scoop.

The concept of scooping had become much more important than eating.

Adults are no different.

There was a very interesting article recently published in **USA Today.** Its title was *"So, How Much Money Does it Take to be Rich?"*

With the publisher's permission, I'm going to quote enough of the article to give you the gist.

> *"Pity the poor millionaire.*
>
> *"Not that Harold Rostow, who has $1 million in stocks and bonds, is hanging on his monthly Social Security checks. The 67-year-old divorced lawyer lives in a $500,000 house in Encino, Calif., drives a Lexus and takes several $8,000 vacations a year ...*
>
> *'It's not where I can take a trip to Europe or Canada for a whole summer,' says the transplanted New Yorker who still works part time. 'A real millionaire could do those things.' ...*
>
> *'If I had another $1 million in stocks and bonds, I'd be in much better shape,' he says ...*

"Don't tell that to Ken Willett of Portland, Ore., a 44-year-old software developer who netted about $2 million when a computer company he helped found went public in 1986.

"Now a consultant, Willett and his wife, Theresa, have about $2 million in liquid assets, plus $2 million in a 6,000-square-foot city house and a beach-front home. Each year, they take a $10,000 vacation with their four kids and give more than $15,000 to charity ...

'With another $2 million in assets,' he says, 'I would worry less, travel a bit more and do more charitable work.' ...

"Stopler (an investment adviser quoted in the article) considers $3 million a pivotal threshold of affluence ...

"Not according to Karen and Tim Faber of Columbia, S.C., who cleared a tidy sum when they sold their personnel staffing company last year. The Fabers have about $3.5 million in investable assets, plus $3.5 million in non-liquid stock ... and Tim says, 'I don't consider ourselves rich. It's just not there yet.'

"He says he probably will reach that magical mark when he can afford a $5 million jet, which would provide more freedom in his business and personal life ...

"PSI Senior Vice President John DeMarco says when you reach $5 million in financial assets, 'You start to see the level of insecurity decrease.' ...

"Yet for most families, DeMarco says, $10 million is the 'real benchmark' of dollar-burning, rolling-in-it wealth."

(Copyright 1997, **USA Today**. Reprinted with permission.)

So how much ice cream do we need in our bowl?

I think Solomon, the richest **and** wisest man that ever lived, must have pondered the same question when he wrote the book of Ecclesiastes. In the twelve short chapters of Ecclesiastes, Solomon used the word meaningless no less than thirty-one times. Referring to himself as the Teacher he begins Ecclesiastes with this statement,

> *"Meaningless! Meaningless!"*
> *says the Teacher.*
> *"Utterly meaningless!*
> *Everything is meaningless."*
> **(Ecclesiastes 1:2)**

That's a pretty blunt message from the richest and wisest man that ever lived. Solomon's story is about having everything: immense wealth, great wisdom and absolute power. His revelation is that even the greatest prizes of men all too soon become meaningless.

> *"I undertook great projects: I built*
> *houses for myself and planted vine-yards.*
> *I made gardens and parks and planted*
> *all kinds of fruit trees in them.*
> *I made reservoirs to water groves of flourishing trees.*
> *I bought male and female slaves*
> *and had other slaves who were born in my house.*
> *I also owned more herds and flocks than anyone in Jerusalem*
> *before me.*
>
> *I amassed silver and gold for myself,*
> *and the treasure of kings and provinces.*
> *I acquired men and women singers, and a harem as well—-*
> *the delights of the heart of man. I became*
> *greater by far than anyone in Jerusalem before me.*
> *In all this my wisdom stayed with me.*

I denied myself nothing my eyes desired;
I refused my heart no pleasure.
My heart took delight in all my work,
and this was the reward for all my labor.
Yet when I surveyed all that my hands had done
and what I had toiled to achieve,
everything was meaningless, a chasing after the wind;
nothing was gained under the sun."
(Ecclesiastes 2:4-11)

Solomon's message is clear. Life apart from God's plan for us is empty and meaningless.

Satan's great lie is that security comes from always seeking a little more than we currently have. He wants us to waste our lives believing that as our assets rise our fears will diminish, that power brings peace to our spirit and that our deepest desires and biggest problems are solved simply by having more.

This quest for abundance is always a trap.

Meaningless.

Ecclesiastes would be a noble book if it did nothing more than expose this great deception.

But, Solomon reveals the truth of life as well.

Life and all that we have is a gift from God. And to those who seek Him comes the divine gift of being satisfied and of truly enjoying what we have, for

"... godliness with contentment is great gain."
(1 Timothy 6:6)

and,

*"A man can do nothing better than to eat and drink
and find satisfaction in his work. This too, I see,
is from the hand of God, for without him, who can eat or
find enjoyment? To the man who pleases him, God gives
wisdom, knowledge and happiness, but to the sinner
he gives the task of gathering and storing up wealth
to hand it over to the one who pleases God."*
(Ecclesiastes 2:24-26)

Five thousand years later Solomon's gardens and fruit trees have withered and died. All of his homes are rubble and the glorious temple he built for the Lord is in ruin. His slaves, wives, servants and friends were laid to rest long ago and all of his immense wealth has been scattered to the four corners of the earth.

But his words of wisdom live on,

*"Now all has been heard;
here is the conclusion of the matter:
Fear God and keep his commandments,
for this is the whole duty of man."*
(Ecclesiastes 12:13)

It's something to think about the next time we reach for the ice cream.

6

The Condition of
Your Flocks — II

Preparing Your Personal
Income Statement

*"A little sleep, a little slumber, a little folding of the hands
and poverty will come on you like a bandit and scarcity
like an armed man."*
(Proverbs 24:33)

T HE *INCOME STATEMENT* is a summary of all
of your income and expense activity for a desig-
nated period of time.

Remember the *Balance Sheet* reflects your
assets and liabilities frozen *at one point in time*, while the *Income
Statement* reflects the activity during a specific *period of time*.

Businesses may prepare *Income Statements* monthly, quarterly or semi-annually, but the point is always the same; the Income Statement answers basic questions such as ... how am I doing? What kind of steward am I? Am I managing what the Lord has entrusted to me in a manner that ensures that my income exceeds my expenses?

The *Income Statement* also reflects important aspects of our character.

How we steward our resources gives insight into our honesty, our integrity, our priorities — in short, our hearts. Stewardship hones character traits ranging from discipline to compassion and reveals what the Lord can entrust to us without compromising our spiritual development or our relationship with Him.

One only has to read the parable of the Ten Minas in **Luke 19** to know that I am not overstating the case for financial stewardship:

> *"A man of noble birth went to a distant country to have himself appointed king and then to return. So he called ten of his servants and gave them ten minas. 'Put this money to work,' he said, 'until I come back.'*
>
> *But, his subjects hated him and sent a delegation after him to say, 'We don't want this man to be our king.'*
>
> *He was made king, however, and returned home. Then he sent for the servants to whom he had given the money, in order to find out what they had gained with it.*
>
> *The first one came and said,*
> *'Sir, your mina has earned ten more.'*
>
> *'Well done, my good servant!' his master replied. 'Because you have been trustworthy in a very small matter, take charge of ten cities.'*

The second came and said,
'Sir, your mina has earned five more.'

His master answered, 'You take charge of five cities.'

Then another servant came and said, 'Sir, here is your mina;
I have kept it laid away in a piece of cloth. I was afraid of you,
because you are a hard man. You take out what you did not put
in and reap what you did not sow.'

His master replied, 'I will judge you by your own words, you
wicked servant! You knew, did you, that I am a hard man, tak-
ing out what I did not put in, and reaping what I did not sow?
Why then didn't you put my money on deposit, so that when I
came back, I could have collected it with interest?'

Then he said to those standing by, 'Take his mina away from
him and give it to the one who has ten minas.'

'Sir,' they said, 'he already has ten!'

He replied, 'I tell you that to everyone who has, more will be
given, but as for the one who has nothing, even what he has will
be taken away.

But those enemies of mine who did not want me to be king
over them — bring them here and kill them in front of me."
(Luke 19:12-27)

The story of the ten minas is a powerful warning to those who would not take seriously the eternal importance of stewardship.

So, how do we begin to develop the characteristics of a good servant?

Initially, I recommend preparing *Income Statements* on a month-ly basis in order to learn more about your spending patterns. The most efficient way to do this is by using simple software such as **Quicken®** to record your income and to pay your bills. At the end of each month a **Quicken®** function will help you to summarize the month's income and spending activity into *Income Statement* format. If you are not yet ready for computerized *Income Statements* then I recommend the simple spreadsheet format found at **Illustration 3**.

You will find it easy to summarize your income and expenses after a couple of months of practice. You will also discover that important patterns regarding your spending habits will emerge. You will learn to analyze and set goals based on these patterns in Chapter 8. For now let's take a look at the Smith Family's *Income Statement*.

THE SMITH FAMILY INCOME STATEMENT

As we previously discussed, Mr. Smith earns $35,000 a year or $2,917 a month. Mrs. Smith earns $24,000 a year or $2,000 a month. They also earn $20 a month in interest and dividends from their savings account and stock holdings. **Illustration 3** indicates that the Smith's monthly income totals $4,937 before taxes.

The Smiths then looked through their checkbook and began to organize their monthly expenditures using a simple system I call the Group A, B, C method.

Group A expenses consists of three categories: the tithe, taxes and savings. In **Illustration 3** you can see that the Smiths paid $1,075 in federal and state income taxes in January. However, they paid no tithe and were unable to save any of their earnings.

Group B expenses are those expenses incurred for *needs*. This category includes items such as the cost of housing and housing upkeep, food, clothing, utilities, transportation, medical and dental expenses and basic insurances.

THE SMITH FAMILY INCOME STATEMENT FOR THE MONTH ENDING:	JAN	FEB	MAR
INCOME:			
SALARY HUSBAND	$2,917		
SALARY WIFE	2,000		
INTEREST AND DIVIDENDS	20		
TOTAL INCOME	**4,937**		
GROUP "A" EXPENSES			
TITHE	0		
TAXES	1,075		
SAVINGS	0		
GROUP "B" EXPENSES			
FIRST MORTGAGE	(954)		
HOME REPAIR AND MAINTENANCE	(50)		
AUTOMOBILE PAYMENTS	(709)		
AUTO INSURANCE, GAS, REPAIRS, ETC.	(200)		
FOOD	(400)		
CLOTHING	(150)		
GAS, ELECTRICITY, WATER	(150)		
HOMEOWNERS INSURANCE AND TAXES	(150)		
MEDICAL AND DENTAL	(50)		
TELEPHONE	(50)		
OTHER	0		
GROUP "C" EXPENSES			
LIFE INSURANCE	0		
VACATIONS	0		
EDUCATION	(100)		
HEALTH & BEAUTY CARE	(45)		
MISC. EXPENSES	(100)		
ENTERTAINMENT	(150)		
CREDIT CARD PAYMENTS	(275)		
SECOND MORTGAGE	(425)		
FINANCE COMPANY LOAN	(183)		
PARENTS LOAN	0		
OTHER	0		
TOTAL EXPENSES	**(5,216)**		
NET GAIN OR (LOSS) EACH MONTH	**($279)**		

ILLUSTRATION 3

We will call Group A and B expenses *FIXED EXPENSES* because they are for the most part not readily or easily changed. They are considered fundamental living expenses and therefore, we generally have minimal control over them.

Group C expenses are called *VARIABLE EXPENSES*. They refer to expenditures for our *wants*. These may include items such as credit card expenditures, vacations expenses, entertainment expenses, most impulse expenditures, and so-called "necessary" loans that are made solely to enhance lifestyle. Group C expenditures, in short, are for the "niceties" of life. We generally have greater control over the decision to buy or not to buy these items. It is important to realize that it is usually the Group C expenditures, or the *wants* of life, that get most of us into financial difficulty.

Also, note that the distinction between Group B and Group C expenditures is sometimes unclear. One family's *needs* may very well be another family's *wants*. There is nothing inherently wrong with *wants* when your financial house is in order. Once you have surrendered your finances to the Lord, all things are possible. However, we must remember that our ultimate goal is to be good stewards, and **true stewardship begins with total surrender**.

Surrender of your finances to the Lord means turning from rebellion (your will) to submission (His plan). As you surrender, the Lord's abundance is released from His storehouse. His wisdom and financial blessings flow, as promised, to the obedient and trustworthy steward.

> *"I wisdom dwell together with prudence; I possess knowledge and discretion. To fear the Lord is to hate evil; I hate pride and arrogance, evil behavior and perverse speech. Counsel and sound judgment are mine; I have understanding and power ... I love those who love me, and those who seek me find me. With me are riches and honor enduring wealth and prosperity. My fruit is*

**YOUR FAMILY
INCOME STATEMENT
FOR THE MONTH ENDING:**

	JAN	FEB	MAR

INCOME:
SALARY HUSBAND
SALARY WIFE
INTEREST AND DIVIDENDS

TOTAL INCOME

GROUP "A" EXPENSES
TITHE
TAXES
SAVINGS

GROUP "B" EXPENSES
FIRST MORTGAGE
HOME REPAIR AND MAINTENANCE
AUTOMOBILE PAYMENTS
AUTO INSURANCE, GAS, REPAIRS, ETC.
FOOD
CLOTHING
GAS, ELECTRICITY, WATER
HOMEOWNERS INSURANCE AND TAXES
MEDICAL AND DENTAL
TELEPHONE
OTHER

GROUP "C" EXPENSES
LIFE INSURANCE
VACATIONS
EDUCATION
HEALTH & BEAUTY CARE
MISC. EXPENSES
ENTERTAINMENT
CREDIT CARD PAYMENTS
SECOND MORTGAGE
FINANCE COMPANY LOAN
PARENTS LOAN
OTHER

TOTAL EXPENSES

NET GAIN OR (LOSS) EACH MONTH

ILLUSTRATION 4

*better than fine gold; what I yield surpasses choice silver. I walk
in the way of righteousness, along the paths of justice, bestowing
wealth on those who love me and making their treasuries full."*
(Proverbs 8:12-21)

With an attitude of prayer and surrender begin to prepare your
Income Statement.

Take a look at the Smith Family's *Income Statement* in
Illustration 3 and then begin to prepare your family's *Income
Statement* using the format provided for you in **Illustration 4**.
Remember that an *Income Statement* covers a *period of time*, I suggest
that you initially prepare yours on a monthly basis.

After you have completed your *Balance Sheet* and your *Income
Statement* Chapter 8 will instruct you on how to analyze financial
statements to determine your financial strengths and weaknesses.
Chapter 10 will teach you how to set goals in order to correct weaknesses and how to prepare a flexible budget.

7

Monopoly

Remains of the Day

D R. JAMES DOBSON, host of the radio show, *"Focus on the Family,"* is one of the people whom I respect most in this world. He tells a story of an event in his life that is almost identical to my own experience.

My wife's family loves to get together and play board games. They eat, talk and enjoy one another while not really paying much attention to the game at hand. I can't stand it. But, one night they pulled out my game: MONOPOLY®.

Now this was a game I could sink my teeth into. This was real life. I played intensely, buying property and houses as fast as I could. My houses were replaced by hotels, and soon I controlled most of the board. The first person I forced out of the game was my wife's 80-year-

(Reprinted with permission from, Robert Katz, **The Family Practitioner's Survival Guide to the Business of Medicine**, page 161, ©1998, Aspen Publishers, Inc.)

old grandmother. She never stood a chance. I was ruthless. One by one I picked off the other players until each of them threw their cards and money at me and left the room. Disgusted with my play, they all had quit and left me alone to clean up the pieces.

But, I had won.

As I sat there with my empty victory, it came to me: it all goes back into the box at the end of the game. No matter how hard you play, all the cash, the property, the buildings, everything we own goes back into the box. And, then someone else comes along to play the game.

In the end, it is our relationships with our friends, family and the Lord that counts. What did we do with the people He put into our lives? How well did we love?

The game will go on without us.

How is your game going?

8

Confessions of a Balance Sheet

Wise Analysis
Breaks Financial Paralysis

"A discerning man keeps wisdom in view,
but a fool's eyes wander to the ends of the earth."
(Proverbs 17:24)

AN AIRLINE PILOT, after several years of training and hard work, had finally attained his life-long dream: piloting jumbo jets. As he got into the captain's chair on his first day at his new job, he couldn't help but be impressed by the complexity of the cockpit. As he guided the plane down the runway and into its take-off, he knew that he had truly become a master of technology.

Unfortunately, a few hours after take-off his plane was struck by lightning. In a somber tone the pilot told his passengers, "I have some good news and some bad news. The bad news is we've been struck by lightning and our communications have been knocked out. Fuel is running low, our guidance systems aren't working, and we are hopelessly lost."

The passengers waited.

"The good news is that there is a strong tail wind and we are making great time."

How many of us feel like that pilot? Too often I encounter hard-working, well-trained people working at a feverish pace. Yet, like the pilot, many times they have no idea where they are headed.

In Chapter 4 we learned that building a solid foundation for your personal finances is a two-step process. The first step was to organize your financial situation by preparing your own *Balance Sheet* and *Income Statement*.

The second step of the process is learning how to analyze your financial statements and making the necessary adjustments of good stewardship.

Analyzing your financial statements will help you accomplish three goals:

1. You will identify your financial strengths and weaknesses.

2. You will learn to budget.

3. You will establish short- and long-term financial goals.

ANALYSIS

> *"A man who has riches without understanding*
> *is like the beasts that perish."*
> **(Psalms 49:20)**

God wants you to understand your financial situation and to take charge of it. He wants you delivered from the bondage of constant financial worry and fear and free to use your time and talents for the glory of His kingdom. Financial understanding begins with analysis.

Your analysis should begin with the six sections of the *Balance Sheet*: current assets, fixed assets, other assets, current liabilities, long-term debts and net worth. Here are a few simple rules for analyzing your *Balance Sheet*.

RULE #1

No section of your *Balance Sheet* stands alone.

Each *Balance Sheet* section is affected by all of the others as well as by what takes place in your *Income Statement*. Understanding this interrelationship is a fundamental aspect of financial wisdom. The truth is that there are really only two financial problems in life: a poor current ratio and a poor long-term debt ratio. They both can be detected through a simple analysis of your balance sheet. By calculating these two simple ratios you can monitor your financial health and know exactly what action to take when financial problems occur.

A. THE CURRENT RATIO

The first step in the analysis process is to calculate your current ratio. Look at the *Current Assets* and the *Current Liabilities* sections of your *Balance Sheet*. The current ratio equals *Current Assets* divided by *Current Liabilities*:

CURRENT RATIO =
CURRENT ASSETS divided by CURRENT LIABILITIES

Now, look at the Smith Family's *Balance Sheet*. The Smith's *Current Assets* are $9,500 and their *Current Liabilities* are $18,200 for a current ratio of approximately 52%. That is, for every 52 cents the Smiths have in *Current Assets*, they have $1.00 in *Current Liabilities*. Or expressed in another fashion the Smith's *Current Liabilities* exceed *their Current Assets* by $8,700. This is our first indication that the Smiths may be having financial problems.

RULE #2

Your current ratio should always be greater than 100%, or *Current Assets* must always exceed *Current Liabilities*.

The more your *Current Assets* exceed your *Current Liabilities* the better your financial condition. By how much should your *Current Assets* exceed your *Current Liabilities*? Here are some good rules of thumb.

RULE #3

Your *Current Assets* should be at least twice as large as your *Current Liabilities*, that is, the ratio should be at least 200%. In other words, you should have $2 of *Current Assets* for each $1 of *Current Liabilities*.

RULE #4

Your *Current Assets* should exceed *Current Liabilities* by at least three months of gross wages (gross wages are earnings before taxes):

CURRENT ASSETS *minus* CURRENT LIABILITIES = 3 MONTHS GROSS WAGES

Let's look at the Smith's *Balance Sheet* again. Notice that their *Current Assets* do not even equal, let alone exceed, their *Current Liabilities*. A poor current ratio is almost always a sign of trouble. The symptoms of a poor current ratio are:

- Never having enough money to pay bills at the end of the month.
- Never having anything saved for emergencies.
- Having to charge items to postpone paying for them.
- Taking out loans to pay off charge account balances.
- "Rolling" charge account balances from one charge card to another.

If you have any of these symptoms, you more than likely have, a poor current ratio. Correcting a poor current ratio involves a three-step process.

First, write down your goals and post them where you will see them often. Examples might be:

- My *Current Assets* will exceed my *Current Liabilities* by three months salary within 24 months, or
- My *Current Liabilities* will be entirely paid off within 18 months.

Second, devise a plan to increase your *Current Assets*. We will discuss goal setting and budgeting in more detail in Chapter 10, but for now you need to know that solving financial problems is not simply a mathematical process. A lasting change in your financial situation will be the fruit of developing Godly self-discipline and obedience. We must develop financial self-discipline in order to maintain victory in the face of constant temptation. God's word warns us:

> *"He who ignores discipline comes to poverty and shame,*
> *but whoever heeds correction is honored."*
> **(Proverbs 13:18)**

This leads us to our **third** step: devising a plan to **reduce and control** your *Current Liabilities*. *Current Liabilities* have no real asset associated with them. An automobile loan and a mortgage on a home are both examples of long-term debts that are directly associated with valuable assets, i.e., your car and home. Whereas, *Current Liabilities* are debts usually associated with consumed items such as travel, entertainment, clothes and other non-essential *wants*.

Liabilities that are not directly associated with an asset can be like a rapidly spreading cancer. Before you even realize it, they consume more and more of your earnings. The result being that you have no *Current Assets*. The Bible clearly cautions us:

> *"The borrower is servant to the lender."*
> **(Proverbs 22:7)**

Credit card debts are usually the worst offender. They pull you deeper and deeper into a black hole of debt and virtually destroy your ability to become good stewards. Credit cards should come with the warning: CAN BE HAZARDOUS OR EVEN FATAL TO YOUR FINANCIAL HEALTH.

Now, look at your current ratio. If you see problems you must immediately take the following actions:

1. Freeze all of your *Current Liability* accounts. Under no circumstances should you take on any more *Current Liabilities*.

2. Sit down with your spouse if you are married and work out a plan to pay off your *Current Liabilities* until you have obtained an acceptable current ratio. Commit to eventually being able to pay off your credit card balances at the end of each month.

3. If you can't control your credit card spending, walk into your kitchen, find a nice sharp pair of scissors and *cut them up*. I did this several years ago. The only cards I carry are the ones that insist on full payment at the end of each month. I have never missed the other cards nor the 18%+ annual interest they charge.

4. Once you have your current ratio under control monitor it and insist that your *Current Assets* always exceed your *Current Liabilities* ... the more the better. Strive to exceed the boundaries suggested by these rules.

The reason I have placed such emphasis on the current ratio is that a strong current ratio implies an abundance of *Current Assets*. With more current assets you will be able to:

- Earn additional income
- Purchase fixed assets
- Meet long-term financial goals
- Be prepared for financial emergencies

B. THE LONG-TERM DEBT RATIO

Our second *Balance Sheet* test is determined by looking at the ratio between your *Fixed Assets* and *Other Assets* divided by your *Long-Term Debts*.

BALANCE SHEET ANALYSIS

THE CURRENT RATIO:

(A) TOTAL CURRENT ASSETS   _____

(B) TOTAL CURRENT LIABILITIES   _____

CURRENT RATIO (A divided by B)   _____

NOTES: _____
_____
_____
_____

GOALS: _____
_____
_____
_____

THE LONG-TERM DEBT RATIO:

(C) FIXED & OTHER ASSETS   _____

(D) LONG-TERM DEBTS   _____

LONG-TERM DEBT RATIO (C divided by D)   _____

NOTES: _____
_____
_____
_____

GOALS: _____
_____
_____
_____

ILLUSTRATION 5

LONG-TERM DEBT RATIO =
FIXED + OTHER ASSETS
divided by LONG-TERM DEBTS

Two rules govern this relationship:

RULE #5

The value of your *Fixed Assets* and *Other Assets* should always exceed the value of your *Long-Term Debts*.

RULE #6

The amount of your wages consumed by *Long-Term Debt* payments should not exceed 35% of your gross income.

Let's look at the Smith Family again (**Illustrations 1 and 3**). The sum of their *Fixed Assets* and *Other Assets* is $271,700 which exceeds their *Long-Term Debts* of $192,000. This is good, they have complied with Rule #5. However, the sum of their mortgages and auto payments is $2,088 which is 42% of their gross income. Because this exceeds the 35% guideline, they have failed to comply with Rule #6. This is another confirmation that the Smiths are probably feeling a financial strain.

Using **Illustration 5**, calculate your family's current ratio and long-term debt ratio. What do these ratios say about your present financial situation?

Once you have analyzed your *Balance Sheet* and determined if there are problem areas, Chapter 10 will discuss the problem solver, the *Income Statement*.

9

Scrooge

Turned Off to Tithing

B Y THE TIME FRANK HAD BECOME A CLIENT of mine he had been seeing a psychiatrist several times a week for over twenty years.

As best as I could determine it was never a question of sanity, it was more a matter of loneliness. Over the decade that I worked with Frank I came to realize that the only people that ever talked to him were those that were paid for it.

There were the employees that he terrorized. Their conversations were short and to the point. They had all been the victims of his demeaning outbursts at one time or another, so their goal was to be in and out of his presence as quickly as possible.

There was Frank's family. To no one's surprise he was divorced. There was, however, a steady string of girl friends, each staying just long enough to get a new car or a new house and then, quickly having had their fill of him, they bolted for the nearest exit. His children visited at Christmas because he agreed to pay for all of their travel expenses and to give them a large check for showing up.

The only other people that he ever spoke to were his financial advisors, like me his CPA, or his attorney or a few others who came by occasionally for business purposes.

Although Frank owned a lake-front mansion that had cost well over a million dollars to build, it sat empty and unoccupied. I would always meet with him in a small, dimly lit, sparsely furnished second home where he resided and conducted business.

Our meetings had become predictable. Early each year I would drive to his home to help him gather the information necessary to pre-pare his income tax returns. But, before we could begin that process he would always say to me, "Come here. I want to show you some-thing."

And with an air of great secrecy he would reach down into the bot-tom drawer of his desk and pull out an old handwritten journal which he used to track his worth.

"Look here." He'd point to a column of numbers that he had scrawled on the ledger page. Today he valued himself at eight million dollars.

"And look here." Then he'd point to last year's column of figures, when he had only been worth six million dollars.

Then he'd say, "Not bad." It was never a question, it was always a statement of fact that he shared with me as he put the journal back into the desk drawer.

We'd press on with his tax return and to the inevitable question I would ask every year about charitable contributions, which would always be answered with his opium of the masses lecture.

It went something like, "If they weren't so lazy ... get off their rears and get a job ... and the churches are worst of all ... charlatans ... thieves ... there is no God ... just weak people who need a myth ..."

Dealing with Frank was an arduous task, but one thing was for sure, I was never confused as to where he stood on the topic of charitable giving. What baffles me is that the feelings Frank so proudly proclaimed are apparently silently shared by many.

Our firm prepares hundreds of tax returns each year and I can count on two hands, maybe one, the number of individuals who tithe. And, it's not just my clients. Every statistic I have read on the subject of giving indicates that only about three percent of the population tithes. It's perplexing.

Perplexing because the Lord makes it crystal clear that tithing is important to Him.

In fact it is so important to God that He not only commands us to tithe, but He counsels us regarding the attitude with which we are to tithe. He then describes in great detail the promises awaiting the faithful tither in His storehouse.

He commands us in the book of Leviticus,

> *"A tithe of everything from the land, whether grain*
> *from the soil or fruit from the trees,*
> *belongs to the Lord; it is holy to the Lord."*
> **(Leviticus 27:30)**

And Jesus reiterates the requirement in the gospel of Matthew,

> *"Woe to you, teachers of the law*
> *and Pharisees, you hypocrites!*
> *You give a tenth of your spices — mint, dill and cumin.*
> *But you have neglected the more important*
> *matters of the law — justice, mercy and faithfulness.*

You should have practiced the latter,
without neglecting the former."
(Matthew 23:23)

Now, there are many times in the Bible when the Lord demands obedience, period. Moses is commanded to go to pharaoh, Jonah likewise to Nineveh, and Gideon to attack the Midianites almost single handedly. However, on the subject of tithing, the command is coupled with an attitude requirement as well,

"Each man should give what he has decided in his heart to
give, not reluctantly or under compulsion,
for God loves a cheerful giver."
(2 Corinthians 9:7)

With the proper attitude God even promises great reward:

"Bring the whole tithe into the storehouse,
that there may be food in my house.
Test me in this, says the Lord Almighty,
and see if I will not throw open the floodgates of heaven
and pour out so much blessing
that you will not have room enough for it."
(Malachi 3:10)

"Remember this: whoever sows sparingly will also
reap sparingly, and whoever sows generously
will also reap generously."
(2 Corinthians 9:6)

"Give and it will be given to you:
good measure, pressed down, shaken together,
running over, will be poured into your lap.
For by your standard of measure
it will be measured to you in return."
(Luke 6:38)

That's powerful stuff.

And so I find myself back at my original point of confusion as I wonder why the Lord gives us such detailed instructions regarding tithing? And, why are we so reluctant to follow His instructions?

Clearly, He doesn't need our money.

Think about it, currency is nothing more than a dead tree that has been pulverized, pressed out and printed with ink. History has shown us that it is easily inflated or deflated into worthlessness. And, you surely can't eat it when times are tough.

So why make a fuss about tithing? Why the commands and the detailed explanations? Why the promise of great rewards? What is God trying to teach us?

I believe that He is trying to save us from ourselves. God continues to reach out to us prying our choking hands of self from around our hearts.

Self-sufficient,

self-righteous,

self-protecting,

self-indulgent

and self-loving hands

prevent us from feeling His loving touch.

With the tithe God begins to remove our hands from our hearts and our thoughts from ourselves, simultaneously transforming our spirit and our flesh through this single act of obedience.

God simultaneously transforms our spirits and our flesh through this single act of obedience. As we tithe, we confess our dependence on God and our spirits grow in faith. By casting our bread upon the water, God not only creates relief for those in need but He also proves His word true by blessing the giver.

Self will always be a lonely room where we sit endlessly trying to calculate our own worth.

Tithing is about the transformation of spirit and flesh.

For years I tried to tell that to Frank, but he thought I needed to see a psychiatrist.

* * * * * * * *

"Command those who are rich in this present world not to be arrogant nor to put their hope in wealth, which is so uncertain, but to put their hope in God, who richly provides us with everything for our enjoyment.
Command them to do good, to be rich in good deeds, and to be generous and willing to share.
In this way they will lay up for themselves as a firm foundation for the coming age, so that they may take hold of the life that is truly life."
(1 Timothy 6:17-19)

10

Income Statement Analysis & Budgeting

God, Caesar and You

BUDGETS ARE LIKE DIETS. Most people hate them and so they usually fail. The reason is logical: human beings are dynamic; our circumstances change from moment to moment and day to day. Budgets on the other hand are often rigid and inflexible. They don't adapt well to real life financial situations and, therefore, are doomed to failure from the onset.

So, if you have tried budgeting and failed, take heart, this chapter is going to introduce you to an easy, flexible budgeting method I call *God, Caesar and You.*

During my career I have spoken with hundreds of people about their financial goals and have found them to be remarkably similar. People want a nice home to live in, to be able to provide for their family's needs, and to be prepared for retirement. Most have long ago established straightforward financial goals and don't realize it.

God, Caesar and You simply says:

1. Analyze your present spending patterns,
2. Realize what your goals are, and
3. Budget toward attaining them.

The purpose of a budget is to take your present *Income Statement* and over time bring it into agreement with an *Income Statement* based on Godly principles.

The reason this is so important is that the *Income Statement* ***builds*** *the Balance Sheet.* When your income exceeds your expenses the effect will be seen in one of two places on your *Balance Sheet.* It will either increase your assets or decrease your liabilities. Understanding this basic concept is crucial. When your income consistently exceeds your expenses, your *Balance Sheet* grows stronger and stronger and your financial house is being constructed on a solid rock foundation. This is a vital principle of stewardship.

The remainder of this chapter will discuss this simple method of analysis and budgeting. **Illustrations 6 and 7** will guide you through this procedure using the Smith Family's *Balance Sheet* and *Income Statement* as examples.

GOD, CAESAR AND YOU

Let's refer to the *Income Statement.* The first and most important group of expenses to be budgeted are Group A expenses. Remember that Group A expenses consist of tithes and offerings (God), taxes (Caesar) and savings (You). These are the expenses that **must** be paid in full, first and at all times:

1. A tithe to the Lord,

2. A tenth to you, and

3. Whatever the tax man demands.

Why a tithe?

Because it honors the Lord's command to us.

As we saw in Chapter 9, tithing is very important to the Lord. So much so that He even instructs us as to the manner in which we are to tithe and tells us what we can expect to receive as a result of our obedience.

Understand this: God who owns everything does not need our tithe. The purpose of the tithe is to develop Godly discipline, character and obedience in us. As we trust and allow Him to develop these qualities in our lives, we begin to discover that the floodgates of heaven do in fact open up.

The command to tithe is found at *Leviticus 27:30*,

> *"A tithe of everything from the land, whether grain from the soil or fruit from the trees, belongs to the Lord;*
> *it is holy to the Lord."*

The Lord also instructs us to have a good attitude about tithing.

> *"Each man should give what he has decided in his heart to give,*
> *not reluctantly or under compulsion,*
> *for God loves a cheerful giver."*
> **(2 Corinthians 9:7)**

> *"Remember this: whoever sows sparingly will also reap sparingly,*
> *and whoever sows generously will also reap generously."*
> **(2 Corinthians 9:6)**

And the Lord reveals the blessings in store for those who tithe.

"Bring the whole tithe into the storehouse, that there may be food in my house. Test me in this, says the Lord Almighty, and see if I will not throw open the floodgates of heaven and pour out so much blessing that you will not have room enough for it."
(Malachi 3:10)

"Give and it will be given to you: good measure, pressed down, shaken together, running over, will be poured into your lap. For by your standard of measure it will be measured to you in return."
(Luke 6:38)

You'd think we'd be racing down the aisle every Sunday with our tithe — so clear is the word of God regarding its power and promise. Yet, less than five percent of all Christians tithe.

It has been my personal observation as a practicing CPA for almost twenty-five years that clients with severe financial problems do not tithe. Coincidence? I doubt it.

I'll be honest with you, tithing was very hard for me to do at first. I'd start to write a check and my hand would almost freeze up. I'd question the Lord, "Oh, Lord do you really want me to tithe? Isn't that just for Old Testament times?"

I could feel Him smile.

I'd criticize his ministers. "Look how they're wasting (or worse) the money!"

Again, He'd smile.

I'd bargain.

"Lord, how about 10% of my income after taxes?"

Finally, I surrendered. And, do you know what happened? The "pressed down, shaken together, running over" promises of Luke 6:38 happened! My businesses have thrived, my personal finances are solid, and more importantly, my spirit has grown as He has developed in me the heart of a cheerful giver.

There is no compromise to the tithe.

The next budget item is saving 10% for yourself. Americans are notorious for how little we save. The average American saves less than 1% of his or her salary while the average Japanese citizen saves close to 20%. The only way to strengthen your balance sheet is by saving. Saving increases your *Current Assets*. As *Current Assets* grow they can be converted to *Fixed Assets* and *Other Assets*, both of which contribute to a greater net worth.

The Final Group A expense is taxes. We live in the greatest country that has ever existed and we have an obligation to support its operation. Jesus tells us in **Matthew 22:21**,

> *"Render to Caesar the things that are Caesar's, and to God the things that are God's."*

So we should pay our taxes and pray for God to guide our leaders in spending them wisely.

Group A expenses should consume approximately 40% of your gross income.

The remaining 60% of your income must be prioritized to first pay Group B expenditures. Any remaining funds can be applied to Group C expenditures. How this is accomplished is up to you. Remember to keep it flexible and to seek the Lord's guidance, discernment and discipline.

Let's look at our case study, the Smith's.

Using **Illustration 5** the Smiths analyzed their *Balance Sheet* and determined the root of their financial problems. What they discovered was that their *Current Liabilities* far exceeded their *Current Assets* and that too much of their income was going to pay *Long-Term Debts*.

Their financial problems were now clear.

Their next step was to develop a budget using their *Income Statement* to solve their problems. **Illustration 6** displays the Smith's current *Income Statement* and the budget goals they established. Their budget goals were established by taking a hard look at how their money was being spent and then reallocating their expenditures using the *God, Caesar and You* method.

Starting with Group A expenditures the Smiths listed their budget goals as follows:

1.   They are going to tithe

2.   They are going to apply 10% of their wages initially to debt reduction. Once their debts are under control that 10% will go into a savings account. The Smiths are committed to paying off their balances on their credit cards and their finance company loan within 24 months.

3.   They are going to sell their boat in order to pay off their second mortgage.

4.   After learning about different types of insurance and then reviewing their automobile insurance policy, they decided to increase their deductible, thereby reducing their transportation cost by fifty dollars a month. (Insurance needs will be discussed in Chapter 18.)

5.   They are going to cash in their whole life insurance policies and replace them with term insurance. The cash surrender value they receive will be used to pay back

their parents the $2,000 owed them, and the balance will be applied against credit card debt.

6. They are going to reduce their entertainment expenditures to $50 a month and take the remaining $100 a month and put it into an account which will be used for an annual vacation.

The Smiths have established very reasonable budget goals which will deliver them from their financial problems and lay the foundation for a strong financial future. **Illustration 7** shows what the Smith's financial statement will look like in two years.

Remember, ultimately a budget is only as good as the discipline behind it,

"Whoever loves discipline loves knowledge."
(Proverbs 12:1)

"No discipline seems pleasant at the time, but painful. Later on, however, it produces a harvest of righteousness and peace for those who have been trained by it."
(Hebrews 12:11)

Before we move on to another very important aspect of improving your *Income Statement*, let's review what we just learned.

1. Analyze your *Balance Sheet* by calculating your current ratio and your long-term debt ratio to isolate your financial weakness (see **Illustration 5**).

2. Use your *Income Statement* to attack financial weaknesses. Do this by setting budget goals using the *God, Caesar and You* expenditure method.

3. Pray that the Lord will supernaturally grant you the discipline and perseverance that you need to break financial bondage.

THE SMITH FAMILY
INCOME STATEMENT
AND BUDGET GOALS TO ATTAIN IN 24 MONTHS

	JAN	BUDGET GOALS
INCOME:		
SALARY HUSBAND	$2,917	$3,300
SALARY WIFE	2,000	2,100
INTEREST AND DIVIDENDS	20	20
TOTAL INCOME	4,937	5,420
GROUP "A" EXPENSES"		
TITHE & OFFERINGS	0	(600)
TAXES	(1,075)	(1,100)
SAVINGS	0	0
GROUP "B" EXPENSES		
FIRST MORTGAGE	(954)	(954)
HOME REPAIR AND MAINTENANCE	(50)	(50)
AUTOMOBILE PAYMENTS	(709)	(709)
AUTO INSURANCE, GAS, REPAIRS, ETC.	(200)	(150)
FOOD	(400)	(400)
CLOTHING	(150)	(150)
GAS, ELECTRICITY, WATER	(150)	(150)
HOMEOWNERS INSURANCE AND TAXES	(150)	(150)
MEDICAL AND DENTAL	(50)	(50)
TELEPHONE	(50)	(50)
OTHER	0	0
GROUP "C" EXPENSES		
LIFE INSURANCE	0	(50)
VACATIONS	0	(100)
EDUCATION	(100)	(100)
HEALTH & BEAUTY CARE	(45)	(45)
MISC. EXPENSES	(100)	(100)
ENTERTAINMENT	(150)	(50)
CREDIT CARD PAYMENTS	(275)	0
SECOND MORTGAGE	(425)	0
FINANCE COMPANY LOAN	(183)	0
PARENTS LOAN	0	0
OTHER	0	0
TOTAL EXPENSES	(5,216)	(4,958)
NET GAIN OR (LOSS) EACH MONTH	($279)	$462

THIS WILL NOW BE PUT INTO A SAVINGS ACCOUNT

ILLUSTRATION 6

THE SMITH FAMILY
BALANCE SHEET
DECEMBER 31, 20XX + 2 YRS.

ASSETS		LIABILITIES & NET WORTH	
CURRENT ASSETS		**CURRENT LIABILITIES**	
CASH	$5,000	CREDIT CARD DEBT	$0
BANK SAVINGS ACCOUNT	5,000	FINANCE COMPANY LOAN	0
STOCK MUTUAL FUNDS	5,000		
TOTAL CURRENT ASSETS	**15,000**	**TOTAL CURRENT LIABILITIES**	**0**
FIXED ASSETS		**LONG-TERM DEBTS**	
RESIDENCE	180,000	FIRST MORTGAGE	118,000
AUTOMOBILES	20,000	SECOND MORTGAGE	0
FURNITURE, FIXTURES		AUTO LOANS	20,000
& PERSONAL EFFECTS	25,000	LOAN FROM PARENTS	0
TOTAL FIXED ASSETS	**225,000**	**TOTAL LONG-TERM DEBTS**	**138,000**
OTHER ASSETS		**TOTAL LIABILITIES**	**138,000**
LIFE INSURANCE CASH	0		
SURRENDER VALUE			
401 (K) PLAN	30,000		
PENSION PLAN	14,000		
TOTAL OTHER ASSETS	**44,000**	**NET WORTH**	**146,000**
TOTAL ASSETS	**$284,000**	**TOTAL LIABILITIES & NET WORTH**	**$284,000**

ILLUSTRATION 7

**Note: Compare the Smith's Net Worth now to their net worth
2 years earlier in Illustration 1.**

Now it is time we moved beyond our talk about budgeting and controlling expenses. Many books on financial planning never address an equally important aspect of improving your net worth, that is increasing your income.

STEP OUT AND PROSPER!

There are more alternatives available to you than just cutting expenses.

1. How about a raise? A good Christian worker should be rewarded for his 100% efforts coupled with a good attitude. If you deserve a raise ask for it.

    "The worker deserves his wages."
    (1 Timothy 5:18)

2. Consider your worth in the present day market. Are you being paid the current market value for your skills? I often see good men and women unhappy in their present work, but too intimidated by a spirit of fear to change jobs. Their fear of change and the illusion of "security" often keeps them settling for less than God's best for them. *Your security is the Lord*, not your job. If you feel led to change jobs, get on your knees in prayer and I assure you that He will guide you into His perfect will for your life. Search the job market, take classes that enhance your skills and continue to pray for guidance. If the job you now have isn't a blessing, there is one out there that is.

3. Self-employment may be the answer for some of you who have always thought about owning your own business. Begin with researching the market you are interested in, talk to people who are self-employed and get

council from an attorney or a CPA. Above all, seek God and trust Him for supernatural guidance and blessings. He's a good God who wants to give His children good gifts.

PART
II

Give Portions to Seven, Yes Eight

11

Before We Begin

A Word or Two
About Investing

AH, THE PERILS OF INVESTING. Do you remember what happened to the poor servant who buried his master's money instead of investing it?

"His master replied, 'You wicked, lazy servant! So you knew that I harvest where I have not sown and gather where I have not scattered seed? Well then, you should have put my money on deposit with the bankers, so that when I returned I would have received it back with interest.

Take the talent from him and give it to the one who has the ten talents. For everyone who has will be given more, and he will have an abundance. Whoever does not have, even what he has

will be taken from him. And throw that worthless servant
outside, into the darkness, where there will be
weeping and gnashing of teeth."
(Matthew 25:26-30)

Investment decisions cause many people to weep and gnash their teeth, or worse.

Investing used to be simple. Banks offered savings accounts and stockbrokers sold stocks and bonds. That was it.

Now, everyone sells every kind of "financial product" (as they are now called); and they are as varied as the promises made to go with them. You can often borrow money less expensively from your broker than from your banker and buy stocks cheaper from your banker than from your broker. Financial products can even be bought at your local department store or through your credit card company.

What this all adds up to is that there are more people than ever saying, "I am an expert. Give me your money." There are more brokers, bankers, financial planners, web sites, insurance agents, CPAs and attorneys offering more financial *advice* than can be understood in a life time.

So what do you do?

The remaining chapters of this book are dedicated to answering that question in detail. But, before we begin to discuss specific investments, it is necessary that we review some of the fundamentals of investing.

TEN BRIEF, BIBLE-BASED, BASICS OF INVESTING

1. IF IT SOUNDS TOO GOOD TO BE TRUE, IT IS!

*"A simple man believes anything, but a prudent man
gives thought to his steps."*
Proverbs 14:15

"A quick tempered man does foolish things ..."
Proverbs 14:17

2. NEVER buy **any investment** (stocks, bonds, insurance, a house, a certificate of deposit, *any investment*) you do not thoroughly understand. NEVER, EVER buy an investment sold unsolicited over the telephone, television, radio or internet. Do not succumb to high-pressure sales tactics. Sometimes the most prudent investment decision you will ever make is to boldly state, "No, I am not interested."

*"Stay away from a foolish man, for you will not find
knowledge on his lips."*
Proverbs 14:7

*"The first to present his case seems right, till another
comes forward and questions him."*
Proverbs 18:17

3. Build your investment portfolio slowly and consistently. The best way to accomplish this is to discipline yourself to save money from each paycheck and invest it wisely. Do not put off saving until a better time, when you can better afford it. That time will never come. Begin now, little by little.

"... he who gathers money little by little makes it grow."
Proverbs 13:11

4. If you don't have the temperament for a particular investment don't buy it. For example, if you have invested in a stock and find that its day-to-day price fluctuations give you heart palpitations, then you are probably not suited for investing in the stock market. Even if you have discovered this fact about yourself after you have purchased a particular investment it is still probably best for you to sell the investment and learn from your experience.

> *"An anxious heart weighs a man down."*
> ***Proverbs 12:25***

5. Be conservative in your investing. Don't fall for wild stories about doubling and tripling your money in a short period of time. *Home run* stories about people whose stocks went up tremendously in value are great to hear, but in reality seldom exist. *Stupidity* stories are seldom heard, yet exist everywhere. Too many people make poor investment decisions because someone tells them *what they want to hear* and they open themselves up to a spirit of greed.

> *"The discerning heart seeks knowledge, but the mouth of a fool feeds on folly."*
> ***Proverbs 15:14***

> *"A discerning man keeps wisdom in view, but a fool's eyes wander to the ends of the earth."*
> ***Proverbs 17:24***

6. Buy and hold. Most gain comes through long-term growth. If you properly diversify and allocate your assets in the beginning they will bear fruit in due season.

> *"The plans of the diligent lead to profit as surely as haste*
> *leads to poverty."*
> **Proverbs 21:5**

> *"... the desires of the diligent are fully satisfied."*
> **Proverbs 13:4**

7. Monitor your investments and never be afraid to take gains or losses. There is an old stock market adage that applies to all investing: "bulls make money, bears make money and pigs get slaughtered."

> *"A greedy man brings trouble to his family."*
> **Proverbs 15:27**

> *"A prudent man sees danger and takes refuge,*
> *but the simple keep going and suffer for it."*
> **Proverbs 22:3**

8. All investments require thorough knowledge on your part. Never turn your money over to any "expert" and let him or her invest without your knowledge and input. This is turning stewardship of what the Lord has entrusted to you over to someone else and it is not scriptural. Advisors play an important role, they advise, but you make the decisions.

> *"... knowledge comes easily to the discerning."*
> **Proverbs 14:6**

> *"The wisdom of the prudent is to give thought to their ways."*
> **Proverbs 14:8**

9. Don't invest money with someone because they share your race, religion, occupation, club membership, etc. The May 20, 1985 issue of **Forbes Magazine** offered some timeless advice on this subject in an article entitled *The Smarter They Are the Harder They Fall*:

"Con men have learned that churches may be one of the best covers for their schemes. In the last few years Mormons in Utah have lost hundreds of millions to swindlers taking advantage of church connections. In Florida con artists using the title National Institute of Christian Financial Planning Inc. took investors to the cleaners by promising to invest in good works that also would turn a profit.

Ford Oil & Development, Inc. Does the name sound familiar? It is a penny stock company that held its annual meeting in Florida several weeks ago during a three-day fundamentalist religious revival.

The Ford pitch: Drill for oil in Israel guided by scripture. Enforcement officials say brokers were on the scene to take orders. Those not at the revival were encouraged by evangelical radio broadcasts to buy shares. And hundreds, perhaps thousands, of the faithful bought, sending the stock, once a Utah shell company, climbing from 8 cents a share to 48 cents. Recently the price was 17 cents.

Mailing lists, a modern refinement, are great tools for con men. Newsletters entice the faithful by pitching investment through scriptures, pitched to the large audience of fundamentalists in this country who believe Armageddon is at hand.

One such newsletter talked about electronic fund transfer as a device to be used by the coming Antichrist to control the world. Meanwhile, the editor was encouraging readers to invest with him in dicey land and diamond deals as a means of defeating the devil."

*(Reprinted by Permission of **Forbes Magazine** © 2000 1985.)*

"A righteous man is cautious in friendship,
but the way of the wicked leads them astray."
Proverbs 12:26

10. Finally, develop DISCERNMENT. There is absolutely
    no doubt in my mind that the Holy Spirit will guide you
    in your stewardship decisions if you submit them to His
    authority. But, remember that He is a gentlemen and
    He won't take what you will not willingly surrender.
    He reveals truth to those who quietly wait and humbly
    listen for His instruction. Lines like, "It's a great invest-
    ment," "no-risk," "unbelievable rate of return," "can't
    fail," "good as gold," "hurry up or you'll miss out,"
    shouldn't be met with open arms, but rather with open
    skepticism.

"It is not good to have zeal without knowledge,
or to be hasty and miss the way.
A man's own folly ruins his life,
yet his heart rages against the Lord."
Proverbs 19:2-3

"My son preserve sound judgement and discernment,
do not let them out of your sight;
they will be life for you."
Proverbs 3:21-22

I have heard far too many stories that start out with
great promises and end up as tragic tales of economic
loss. People work so hard for their money and unfortunately part with it far too easily.

If all of this sounds like little more than common sense, it is.
Common sense, discernment, wisdom, understanding and patience
are the fundamental tools of successful investing.

As you consider an investment, any investment, stop and realize what is actually happening. The Lord has entrusted some of His possessions to you for stewardship and like the servant in the parable, your decisions have eternal consequences. Take all of your decisions to the Lord for confirmation before you carry them out. Only after He has confirmed a decision should you proceed to actually invest.

"A wise son heeds his father's instruction."
Proverbs 13:1

"Commit to the Lord whatever you do,
and your plans will succeed."
Proverbs 16:3

(Portions of this chapter were adapted from, Robert Katz, ***The Family Practitioner's Survival Guide to the Business of Medicine***, pages 137-148, ©1998, Aspen Publishers, Inc.)

12

Monopolife

Your Time or Your Money?

"**L**IVE! FROM LAS VEGAS, Nevada, it's America's number one game show, where the question is, 'Are you ready to risk it all?'

"I'm Johnny McDougal, the voice of *Monopolife*, welcoming you once again to the number one rated show on television. In just a moment I will introduce you to tonight's contestants, but first let's meet the man who needs no introduction, our master of ceremonies, Mr. *Monopolife* himself, Ted Mayor."

Johnny McDougal's perfect voice could be counted on to work the audience into a frenzy, and tonight was no exception. As the audience squealed and theme music ascended to the rafters, Ted Mayor bounded out of the darkness and onto center stage. The audience jumped from their seats as the applause continued, and with a well-rehearsed humble gesture, Ted slowly lowered his arms bringing silence to the arena as they waited for his words. Only Ted Mayor, host of America's favorite game show, could say the word "all" stretching it into several sing-song syllables, each making him the center of attention.

"Allllll ... right, Johnny, can you introduce us to today's contestants?"

"I sure can, Ted. Today we've got two tough competitors. Mack Alton from Oklahoma City, Oklahoma and Mary Schrib from Newark, New Jersey. Let's give them both a big *Monopolife* welcome."

From the dark wings of the theater two contestants emerged onto the brightly lit stage. They appeared to be a little overwhelmed by the applause and slightly blinded by the lights. Somewhat dazed by it all they walked straight into Ted Mayor's famous bear hug. He squeezed them like long-lost family members and then with one arm around each contestant guided them to their places on the set.

"Contestants, I want to personally wellllll...come you to *Monopolife*. I know that you both have been instructed on how the game is played and that you've signed your player's contracts. But, let me go over the rules one more time just in case there is one viewer out there, somewhere, in some god-forsaken land who hasn't seen the show.

"You have two wheels in front of you. One is Money, the other is Time.

"First, you spin the Money Wheel and you win the prize it lands on. You can win big cash, real estate, stocks, bonds, gold, silver, even a mansion ... remember *Monopolife* is ...," Ted paused and turned to the audience with a big smile and jabbed the microphone at them. On cue they responded, "THE SHOW OF UNTOLD WEALTH!"

"That's right, UNTOLD WEALTH. But, then ... you must spin the Time Wheel. The Time Wheel has time spaces on it ranging from one hour to ten years. And of course there is also ...," again, Ted pointed the microphone at the audience. This time a more somber chorus sang back, "THE BLACK SPACE!"

Ted resumed, "The time you acquire on the Time Wheel is added to your present age. At the end of the show you leave with all of your wealth ... and all of the time it takes to acquire it. The winner of the game is the player who has acquired the most wealth but has taken the fewest years from his life. Now let's meet our contestants."

"Mack Alton, it says here that you are from Oklahoma. Can you tell the audience a little about yourself?"

"Sure, Ted. I've been married for six years and I sell wholesale paper products. My beautiful wife and kids are in the audience tonight and I'm ready to do whatever it takes to win *Monopolife*."

"Allllllll ... right, Mack, it sounds as if you are ready to play for keeps. Tell us, if you win UNTOLD WEALTH, what are you going to do with it?"

Mack looked down at his hands on the podium. This wasn't a question that he had ever seriously considered, until he was selected as a contestant. His forehead was already starting to bead with perspiration.

"I've been reading a lot of books lately, Ted. I've been reading on business and finance and economics. It's all very confusing, but I guess I'd buy a new house and travel and spend more time with my family. I just want the good life."

"Well, we wish you luck, Mack. Our other contestant comes to us from the Garden State. Mary Schrib, are you ready to risk it all ?"

"I sure am, Ted."

"Mary Schrib, tell the audience a little about yourself."

"I'm married and I have a full time career trading bonds for a large international brokerage firm."

"Well, Mary, that job of yours sounds like great training for managing your wealth."

"It is, Ted. I don't have to study business books to know what I am going to do with my winnings. I deal with wealthy people everyday, and I'm going to leave here tonight just like one of them." Mary shot a glance at Mack. For too many years she'd watched her wealthy clients grow even richer. Tonight was her night, and no paper salesman was going to stand in her way.

"Allll ... right, audience, that sounds like a challenge to me, so let's spin the wheel and start to play *Monopolife*. Mack, you won the toss back stage so you spin first."

Mack reached over to spin the wheel. As he jerked the wheel his hand slipped and he stumbled back. The Money Wheel hummed like the engine of an expensive sports car.

"Thirty thousand dollars! Allll ... right, Mack. You're off to a great start, now spin the Time Wheel."

Mack bent over again. Sweat was stinging the corners of his eyes. He gave the wheel a jerk and crossed the fingers on both hands.

"One year! Not bad, not bad. You can hardly even feel that."

Ted was right — one year was added to Mack's life, not bad for thirty thousand dollars. Mack looked a little heavier, but he felt pretty good.

"Allll ... right, Mary. Give the old Money Wheel a spin."

Not to be outdone, Mary grabbed the wheel, pulled hard and lifted both her hands in victory even before it stopped humming.

"A summer home in Aspen worth TWO MILLION DOLLARS! Oh, oh. I think Mary's come to play!

All right, Mary, spin for Time. Let's see what this is going to cost you?"

Mary reached over with the same confidence, spun the wheel and commanded, "Low Time! Come on Wheel, give me Low Time!"

A groan from the audience let her know it wasn't good.

Ted walked over to her and like a father put his arm around her shoulder. "Oh, Mary, you've landed on decade. But don't worry. You're already a millionaire so now all you have to worry about is keeping your wealth safe."

Mary felt a little tired. She was about ten pounds heavier and when she looked into the monitor she noticed that her hair was a little thinner and a little grayer. She'd have to be careful now. The game lasted for half an hour and time was precious.

Mack watched Mary age before his eyes. His shirt stuck to his chest as he reached for the wheel and started it humming once again.

"5000 shares of IBM with a value today of $825,000. That's the way to hit the old baseball out of the park, Mack!"

Not waiting to be told, Mack grabbed the Time Wheel and closed his eyes.

"Five years. Not bad, Mack. If my math is correct that's like earning $165,000 a year. You wouldn't earn that out there, if you really had to work for it, would you?"

I guess not, Mack thought. But he'd entered the game thirty two years old, now five minutes into the game he was thirty eight. He could see that he was beginning to go bald, but he wasn't sure how bad it was because his eyesight wasn't as sharp as it had been earlier.

The minutes passed and both Mack and Mary grew quieter as they accumulated more and more wealth. As the half-hour drew to a conclusion, both players were becoming very wealthy. However, the Wheel of Time had not been kind to either of them. Focused on wealth, time had slipped away from them. Mack was already sixty years old and Mary was sixty-two.

And then it happened.

Mary had just won a private jet. She reached tentatively for the Wheel of Time and barely recognized her own hand. Her flesh had become wrinkled and her fingers were bony. Weakly she gave the wheel a spin.

The audience went deadly silent. Mary screamed as the Wheel stopped at its only black space, "I don't want to play ... take back everything ... I don't want it ...."

"Oh, Mary, I am so sorry, but you know the rules and you did sign the player's contract. You've landed on Time's Up."

Two guards emerged from the darkness just off-stage, each taking one of Mary's arms. She fainted as they dragged her to the Black Room. The stage lights flickered on and off for an instant, but then music bounced new life into the audience. Ted ran over to Mack smothering him in another big bear hug, "We have a winner! Mack, walk down here with me and let the audience see what a winner looks like."

Mack walked slowly to center stage. He was surprised by how much his back hurt.

"Mack, you've won! ... Almost ten million dollars and you're only sixty years old ... plenty of time left to enjoy it. How does it feel to be rich?"

Mack looked out into the audience, but with his old glasses he couldn't see anything. "Where is my family?

"Oh, I am sorry, Mack, but your wife and kids left you about the time you turned fifty-six ... but how does it feel to be so rich?"

Mack shuffled off the stage. The theater pulsated to the theme of *Monopolife* while Johnny McDougal's perfect voice closed the show, "Tune in next week when two new people, just like you, battle for Time and Money."

13

Cash

The Emergency Fund

O NE OF MY BUSINESS PARTNERS was recently teaching his fifteen-year-old son to drive. The young man was doing just fine until he looked up into the rear view mirror and allowed the car to drift off the road. In the blink of an eye there were two flat tires ... the cost to replace and repair, almost six hundred dollars. Stuff happens. It's not a question of if, it's a question of when. People lose their jobs, children get sick and unexpected expenses, like unwelcome guests, come knocking at your door.

One of the foundational elements of financial stewardship is establishing a fund for emergencies. The principle of preparing for difficult times appears in the very first pages of the Bible with the story of Noah:

*"You are to take every kind of food that is to be eaten and store it
away as food for you and for them."*
(Genesis 6:21)

This Biblical principle of establishing a reserve appears once
again in Genesis as we read Joseph's advice to Pharaoh,

*"And now let Pharaoh appoint commissioners over the land to
take a fifth of the harvest of Egypt during the seven years of
abundance. They should collect all the food of these good years
that are coming and store up the grain under the authority of
Pharaoh, to be kept in the cities for food. This food should be held
in reserve for the country, to be used during the seven years of
famine that will come upon Egypt, so that the country may not
be ruined by the famine."*
(Genesis 41:33-36)

In the very first book of the Bible the Lord has provided us with
two poignant illustrations of the need to prepare for the unexpected. Later, these illustrations are summed up in a simple Proverb,

*"Ants are creatures of little strength,
yet they store up their food in the summer."*
(Proverbs 30:25)

The Biblical principle of establishing a reserve for emergencies
is still valid today. However, it is impractical for us to store food,
therefore our reserve is readily available cash. The question then
becomes how much cash should we have in reserve?

Most books on financial planning advise you to have three to six
months of living expenses in an emergency fund. I have not found a
Biblical basis for this rule of thumb. The Bible teaches that Noah
accumulated a year of provisions and that Joseph amassed almost a
year and a half of food in preparation for the hard times. My rec-

ommendation to you is that you accumulate at least twelve months of *living expenses* in an emergency fund.

To determine exactly what your living expenses are go back and look at your *Income Statement*. Decide which expenses are absolutely necessary if you were to lose your job. Separate these essential expenses from those that you can eliminate during difficult times. These essential expenditures are your living expenses. Therefore, if your living expenses are $1,500 per month, your emergency fund should have at least $18,000 in it.

The primary focus for investing your emergency fund should be safety and liquidity. Should you need access to your emergency fund you want the funds in a safe place and readily available. The interest you earn on your emergency fund is not the issue.

There are four basic investments suitable for an emergency fund:

- Savings Accounts
- Money Market Accounts
- Certificates of Deposit
- Money Market Funds

The first three of these investments are offered by banks, credit unions, and savings and loans (thrifts). The money market fund is usually offered by stock brokerage firms and mutual fund companies.

WARNING: *When transacting business with banks, credit unions, and savings and loans, make sure that you deal only with institutions insured by a federal agency. You can confirm that an institution is federally insured by contacting the following agencies:*

For Banks: *Federal Deposit Insurance Corporation (FDIC)*
202-393-8400

For Credit Unions: *National Credit Union Administration*
(NCUA) 202-638-7590

Now, let's analyze emergency fund investments in terms of safety, liquidity and yield.

SAVINGS ACCOUNTS

With the advent of inflation in the 1970s Americans became very aware of the interest rates being paid on their investments and demanded higher rates. Banks, however, were still closely regulated and so there were few investment alternatives available for conservative investors. In 1986 banks were deregulated and allowed to offer a variety of different accounts, each paying higher interest rates than the traditional passbook savings account. These factors caused the passbook savings account to go the way of the typewriter; however, they remain an alternative for the ultra-conservative investor and for teaching children to begin to save.

> **SAFETY** — When discussing safety in this chapter we will assume that you are always dealing with federally insured institutions. Savings accounts in these institutions are insured up to $100,000 and, therefore, they are very safe.

> **LIQUIDITY** — Savings accounts are very liquid, that is, you have easy access to your funds during regular banking hours. You cannot, however, write checks on passbook savings accounts.

> **YIELD** — Banks are no longer regulated as to how much interest they can pay on savings accounts. The interest rates offered can vary widely and are typically low, so it is in your best interest to compare rates at a variety of

institutions. Interest is paid from the date you deposit your funds until the date you withdraw them.

MONEY MARKET ACCOUNTS

Developed in the early 1980s a money market account is a cross between a higher interest paying savings account and a checking account. They offer a nonfluctuating $1 investment value (your principal is never at risk) and a competitive interest rate.

> **SAFETY** — Money market accounts are insured up to $100,000 by federal agencies. Do not confuse money market *accounts* with money market *funds* which are not federally insured.

> **LIQUIDITY** — Generally, there are two ways to gain immediate access to the cash in your money market account. You can write a limited number of checks on the account (usually three per month) or you can transfer cash from your money market account into one of your other accounts within that same financial institution.

> **YIELD** — Money market account interest rates are allowed to "float," therefore, they stay competitive with similar investments at other financial institutions. Your deposits are credited with interest on a daily basis. Most money market accounts require a minimum balance to open the account.

A money market account is one of the better investment options available for your emergency fund.

CERTIFICATES OF DEPOSIT

Once you have accumulated six months of emergency funds in a readily accessible account, you may wish to invest the balance of your emergency fund in an account that pays slightly higher interest such as a certificate of deposit.

SAFETY — Certificates of deposit are insured up to $100,000 by the FDIC or the NCUA and, therefore, are very safe.

LIQUIDITY — Banking institutions can issue CD's with maturities ranging from 7 days up to several years. Usually the longer the investment term of the certificate, the higher the interest rate you earn. It is important to note that if you need your money prior to the maturity date of the certificate of deposit, a penalty will be imposed for the premature withdrawal of your funds. However, if an emergency occurs and you find that you need your money prior to your certificate's maturity date, consider taking out a short-term loan using the certificate as collateral. All banks will be happy to make this type of loan and it will save you from paying the premature withdrawal penalty.

YIELD — The interest rate paid on CD's is unregulated and can vary substantially. Aggressive banks trying to attract new depositors will often offer higher than average interest rates to entice you to open an account with them. Due to the "tax exempt" status of federal credit unions, you will find that they often offer rates on CD's that are as much a one-half percentage point higher than the rates offered by banks. Yield will also vary according to the amount of your deposit, with "Jumbo CD's" ($100,000 or more) paying the top interest rates.

When interest rates are low try to invest in short-term CD's. When interest rates are higher, try to "lock in" the higher interest rate for as long as possible, bearing in mind that these funds still need to be accessible for emergencies.

There are many web sites that track interest rates offered by banks across the country. Charles Schwab & Co. offers one such excellent web site.

MONEY MARKET FUNDS

Stockbrokerage firms and mutual fund companies offer many fine investments. However, only one is suitable for your emergency fund and that is the money market fund. A money market fund is legally a mutual fund. These funds pool the cash of millions of investors and lend it to large corporations, banks and governments on a short-term basis. The earnings on these loans, less the money market fund's management fee, are then credited to your account in the form of dividends.

Theoretically, a money market fund is also based on a nonfluctuating $1 value, however, they are mutual funds, not bank accounts, and there is the remote possibility that you could lose some of your original investment. This has never happened in the history of the money market fund industry and the general consensus among investment advisors is that money market funds are a safe investment.

Initial investment requirements in money market funds can vary from $100 to more than $25,000 depending on the fund and the ancillary services that it may offer. Most money market funds offer check writing services, but many require that checks be written for a minimum amount, usually $250 to $500. Money market funds are regulated by the Securities and Exchange Commission (SEC), but this is no substitution for your own investigation as to which are the better funds. Most major business magazines will periodically publish a listing of the best money market funds. This information is also posted on a variety of financial web sites.

THE SMITH FAMILY
EMERGENCY FUND CALCULATION

	INCOME STATEMENT	EMERGENCY FUND NEEDS
INCOME:		
SALARY HUSBAND	$3,300	
SALARY WIFE	2,100	
INTEREST AND DIVIDENDS	20	
TOTAL INCOME	5,420	0
GROUP "A"EXPENSES		
TITHE	(550)	
TAXES	(1,100)	
SAVINGS		
GROUP "B" EXPENSES		
FIRST MORTGAGE	(954)	954
HOME REPAIR AND MAINTENANCE	(50)	50
AUTOMOBILE PAYMENTS	(709)	709
AUTO INSURANCE, GAS, REPAIRS, ETC.	(150)	150
FOOD	(400)	400
CLOTHING	(150)	
GAS, ELECTRICITY, WATER	(150)	150
HOMEOWNERS INSURANCE AND TAXES	(150)	150
MEDICAL AND DENTAL	(50)	50
TELEPHONE	(50)	50
OTHER		
GROUP "C" EXPENSES		
LIFE INSURANCE	(50)	
VACATIONS	(100)	
EDUCATION	(100)	100
HEALTH & BEAUTY CARE	(45)	
MISC. EXPENSES	(100)	100
ENTERTAINMENT	(50)	
CREDIT CARD PAYMENTS	0	
SECOND MORTGAGE	0	
FINANCE COMPANY LOAN	0	
PARENTS LOAN	0	
OTHER		
TOTAL EXPENSES	(4,908)	$2,863
NET GAIN OR (LOSS) EACH MONTH	$512	

TOTAL EMERGENCY FUND EQUALS 12 MONTHS OF NEEDS = $34,356 (12 X $2,863)

ILLUSTRATION 8

SAFETY — Due to the short-term nature of a money market fund's investments and the relatively conservative nature of what they invest in, almost everyone agrees that they are very safe. Remember, however, that unlike bank money market *accounts*, money market *funds* are not federally insured. For this reason money market funds will usually pay a slightly higher interest rate than money market accounts.

LIQUIDITY — Almost all money market funds offer 24-hour redemption by phone, wire transfer or check.

YIELD — Money market funds are very competitive and offer excellent short-term interest rates. Yields change daily and you can find a listing of current yields for most of the major funds in the Thursday edition of *The Wall Street Journal.*

Money market funds are another excellent investment for a portion of your emergency fund.

Now would be a good time for you and your spouse to calculate the amount needed for your emergency fund. See **Illustration 8** to help you with this calculation.

Finally, remember in Chapter 10 we discussed the importance of saving 10% of your salary each month. This savings should be directed into your emergency fund until you have the appropriate amount stored away for difficult times.

14

Stocks

The Worship of Wall Street

VEN A FUNDAMENTALLY sound concept when carried to an extreme can become dangerous. Stock markets are a fundamentally sound concept. They allow corporations to efficiently raise capital and individuals to share in the economic success of the corporations they believe in. It is this easy access to corporate capital and individual investment opportunity that has set the stage for this country to be the most economically successful nation in the history of the world. Stock markets are a good idea.

But, something has happened over the last twenty years. For many people the stock market has become America's great casino. Just as gaudy neon lights lure gamblers, the raging bull market of Wall Street beckons the unwary investor, "Don't be left behind. Put your money down on any number, uh, I mean stock and watch it multiply before your very eyes. No knowledge required, no wisdom necessary, everyone's a winner."

Almost daily, corporations with little experience and weak business plans place their newly issued stock into the market for sale. And, everyday billions of dollars are invested by investors with little or no concept of what a stock is or whether the purchase they are making is suitable for their needs. And so, we have a fundamentally sound concept being pushed to the extreme by greed. When we reach this extreme, there will be a collapse. A few years ago the Japanese thought that their economy was invincible. Their stock market appeared impenetrable as it climbed towards 30,000. However, it took just a few months for their market to plunge to 12,000. A plunge from which their stock market has not fully recovered.

Am I telling you not to invest in stocks? Not at all. In fact, for most people, one of their "portions of eight" should be some form of high-quality stock investment. The stock market has historically provided a better return on investment than any other class of asset. However, before you buy a single share of stock you must thoroughly understand what you are investing in. The great prophet Hosea warned us and it bears repeating over and over again:

> *"... my people are destroyed from lack of knowledge."*
> ***(Hosea 4:6)***

The purpose of this chapter is to provide you with a basic understanding of what stocks are and how to begin to obtain the knowledge necessary to wisely invest in them.

STOCKS

Someone has a good idea. Sam Walton (the founder of Wal-Mart) thinks people might like stores that offer virtually everything at "everyday low prices." Bill Gates (the co-founder of Microsoft) thinks his software operating system is the best in the world. Starbucks thinks that people would like to sit around and leisurely drink gourmet coffee. All are great concepts, but to bring the concept to reality, the visionary founders of these companies all shared a common need. They needed money and lots of it. In order to raise that money they decided to offer shares of their corporation to the general public. Stocks are nothing more than a fractional ownership interest in a company. The more shares you own, the more of the company you own.

There are two legal classifications for stock.

The first class, and the class you are probably most familiar with, is *Common Stock*.

Common stock represents general ownership in a corporation and usually provides the shareholder with no preferential rights. Common shareholders share in the general success or failure of the companies in which they have invested. If a company is successful the shareholder's financial reward for the risk they have assumed may come in two forms. A shareholder may receive a dividend payment based on the number of shares they own and also share in the growth of the value of those shares. This increase in the value of a stock is generally referred to as a capital gain or capital appreciation.

The second class of stock is *Preferred Stock*. Preferred stock usually guarantees a certain dividend payout which is preferential. This preferential treatment means preferred stockholders will receive their full guaranteed dividend before common stockholders receive any dividends. Preferred stocks are usually purchased by investors who are looking for a steady stream of income.

Common stocks are further defined by dividing them into several categories and sub-categories.

The three basic categories of common stocks are as follows.

Growth Stocks — are those common stocks that have certain economic attributes which lead the prudent investor to believe that this particular stock will outperform other stocks in the same industry. The typical growth stock is a rapidly expanding company which reinvests all of its profits into continued corporate growth. For this reason growth stocks seldom pay dividends, but often reward their investors with substantial increases in the price of the stock.

Income Stocks — are stocks that are known for paying consistent dividends to their shareholders. A good example would be a utility stock. The primary purpose of an income stock is to provide its shareholders with a dependable steam of dividend income. The trade off for the reliable dividend payout is that income stocks often do not provide significant capital appreciation. The value of income stocks usually fluctuates with its dividend payout and therefore is influenced more by inflation and interest rates than by general stock market conditions.

Value Stocks — are those stocks which are believed to be undervalued by prudent investors. An example might be a corporation whose stock price has dropped due to management problems or a poor economy. However, it is believed that the company is now poised to rebound and that the *value* of the stock will rise at a greater rate than normal.

Growth, income and value stocks are further divided into important subcategories with which you should be familiar. These subcategories help to define stocks in terms of specific corporate attributes such as size or industry.

You will often hear stocks referred to as "blue chip," large-cap, mid-cap or small-cap stocks. These classifications refer to the size of a corporation. "Blue chip" is a term used to define a large, well-established, prudently managed corporation. The term "blue chip" has become synonymous with safety and security based on the historical performance of these companies.

Large-cap stocks are the stocks of corporations with over $10 billion dollars in investment capital. Mid-cap stocks have from $1 billion to $10 billion in investment capital and small-cap stocks have less than $1 billion dollars in investment capital. Remember that investment capital is an indication of corporate size and nothing more. Many small-cap companies are extremely successful and will grow to be large-cap companies some day. And, unfortunately, some poorly managed large-cap companies may someday become small-cap companies.

Stocks may also be referred to by their industry. You will often hear stocks referred to as health care stocks, internet stocks, telecommunication stocks, or bank stocks, etc. Again, this type of classification only denotes industry. It is not an indication as to whether a particular stock will be a suitable investment for you.

Having watched individuals and institutions invest in the stock market for over twenty-five years has allowed me to gather a list of guidelines that should be helpful to you:

1. Never, ever, buy stocks on a tip — even from the best of friends.

2. Always do your own research and make your own investment decisions. There is more literature published about stocks than any other investment, so if you are not willing to do your own investment research, you should not invest in individual stocks.

Your research might start with a favorable impression about an industry or product. You should then begin to analyze the individual companies that make up that industry and select a few of the most promising corporations for further research. From your "short list" of corporations, review the history of each company, analyze its financial statements and become familiar with the performance of its management. Purchase a stock only after you have completed your own research and remain impressed by the corporation and its future.

3. Buy "into" a stock. That is, don't spend all of your investment money at once. Buy 50% of the total stock you intend to purchase and wait. If the stock performs as expected, buy another 25% and wait again. If the stock continues to perform well, invest the final 25%.

4. Never buy more stock than you can afford. Don't buy stock on margin (loans from brokerage firms) and never borrow money to buy a stock.

5. Be patient. Without a doubt those investors that follow a *buy and hold* investment philosophy have the best overall performance. Successful investors purchase a diversified portfolio of stocks, periodically review their holdings and ignore the day-to-day and month-to-month fluctuations of the stock market.

Day trading, market timing and short-term trading isn't investing — it's gambling. Sooner or later individuals who believe that they are smarter than the market will meet with disaster. Avoid brokers who recommend these methods for investing.

6. Periodically (perhaps quarterly) monitor your stock portfolio. Each stock should be reviewed and decisions made to buy, sell or hold.

7. Set "stop losses." Choose a point at which you will sell the stock if it goes down. If the stock drops to that point,

sell it. You cannot pick the correct stock 100% of the time and it is always prudent to cut your losses and to let your profits run. All too often I see investors hanging on to their poorly performing stocks in hopes of a rebound and selling their well-performing stocks too soon.

8. Monitor your portfolio in light of the general stock market. You can have the best individual stocks in the world, but if the market is crashing it will usually take your company down with it. However, good stocks *will* weather bad markets, which is another reason to be prudent and patient.

9. Invest in quality stocks traded over the major exchanges such as the New York Stock Exchange or NASDAQ. Avoid "penny stocks." Penny stocks are cheap, relatively unheard of stocks traded on small regional markets which may be easily manipulated. Stay away from them and the brokerage firms that tout them.

10. Only deal with brokerage firms that carry Securities Investor Protection Corporation (SIPC) insurance.

11. Buy and sell stocks in units of 100 shares. I recommend this because the commission expense is less for even "lots" of 100 shares. An "odd lot" charge is assessed when an odd number of shares is purchased.

12. Since you are going to do your own research and decision making, don't be afraid to deal with reputable discount brokers such as Charles Schwab and Co., Inc. or with banks and other financial institutions that will discount your stock buy and sell transactions.

13. Try before you buy. Do some research, pick some stocks and invest some money on paper only. See how you do for a few months before you really use your own money. Don't cheat.

READING THE FINANCIAL PAGE
ON THE STOCK MARKET

52 week high	52 week low	stock	div	Yield %	PE Ratio	NYSE Sales 100's	H	L	L	chg
871/4	62	XOM	1.64	2.1	38	24903	80	76	79	+.5
(a)	(b)	(c)	(d)	(e)	(f)		(g)			(h)

Most local and national newspapers (*The Wall Street Journal,* *The New York Times,* etc.) carry the previous day's stock market trading activity in their financial section. Stocks are listed by alphabetical abbreviations according to the market they are traded on. The illustration above is typical of the information provided in the stock market section of the financial pages. We will select ExxonMobil as our example and look at the information above for the following information:

a. This information tells us the highest and lowest price of ExxonMobil for the previous 52-week period.

b. The abbreviation for the stock, XOM, is the symbol for ExxonMobil.

c. The dividend paid during the most recent four quarters.

d. Yield of the stock. This is determined by dividing the dividend by the most recent closing price.

e. Price to Earnings Ratio (PE Ratio) is the price of the stock divided by the earnings per share. For example if a stock is trading at $10 per share and it earns $1 per share annually, it is said to have 10 to 1 PE ratio. This is important because specific industries tend to have average PE ratios. If you are looking at a specific stock in that industry and it has a lower than average PE ratio it may indicate that the stock is underpriced or that the company is in some sort of trouble. A high PE ratio may indicate that the stock is overpriced or speculative. Upon researching a particular stock, you should be able to find out why a PE ratio is higher or lower than normal.

f. This column tells how many shares were traded that day expressed in 100's.

g. The daily trading range, that is, the highest, lowest and last price of the stock traded that day.

h. Indicates the change in price from the previous day's closing price. Stock prices are quoted in decimals.

After having said all this, the real question is are stocks for you? **The answer is that individual stocks are not suitable for most investors.** Although the stock market has outperformed the corporate and government bond markets over the last 50 years, the sad truth is that the majority of people lose money because they are *playing the stock market.*

Most individual investors do not have the time, knowledge and/or mental discipline to trade stocks. That is why I believe for the average investor their "portion" in the stock market should be represented by investments in *no-load mutual funds.*

MUTUAL FUNDS

Somewhere, some time ago, someone got a bright idea concerning risk sharing and diversification. Prior to this bright idea if you had $5,000 to invest you'd probably be limited to purchasing 1 or 2 stocks. However, if you pooled your money with hundreds of other investors, that pool of funds could now purchase a varied portfolio of stocks and spread the risk of loss accordingly — thus the birth of the mutual fund.

The primary advantage of mutual funds is that they are managed by professional advisors. This relieves the individual investor from having to comb through research on hundreds of individual stocks. However, it is the responsibility of the investor to research the mutual funds they are considering investing in. The good news is that this is a much easier process than individual stock analysis.

Today the mutual fund business is a multi-billion dollar industry offering funds for stocks, bonds, stocks and bonds, and a variety of other specialized investments.

THE BASICS OF MUTUAL FUNDS

MUTUAL FUND STRUCTURE — There are two basic legal classifications for mutual funds.

1. **Open-End Mutual Funds** — Most mutual funds today are open-ended. This means that new fund shares are issued as more and more people contribute money into the fund. Each shareholder owns his or her proportional share of the total mutual fund shares outstanding.

2. **Closed-End Mutual Funds** — A closed-end fund limits the number of shares issued. In order to buy into a closed-end fund you must purchase someone else's existing shares.

MUTUAL FUND PURPOSES

The purpose of a mutual fund is supposed to be clearly stated in its prospectus (a document required by the Securities and Exchange

Commission which outlines important aspects of the fund). Generally, stock funds will have one or a combination of the following purposes:

1. **Growth funds** try to invest in undervalued stocks believed to have the best potential for long-term capital appreciation. These stocks have been researched by the mutual fund managers and based on that research, they believe these stocks will rise the most in price, thereby producing large capital gains. Generally the dividends on these types of stocks are lower than the dividends on an income oriented stock fund.

2. **Equity Income funds**, on the other hand, concentrate on quality stocks with high-dividend yields. These funds provide a stream of income to the shareholder, but generally offer less opportunity for capital growth.

3. **Value Funds** have fund managers who seek out undervalued or low price to earnings ratio stocks in hopes of identifying those stocks that will appreciate at a greater rate than similar stocks.

4. **Industry or Sector funds** specialize in specific industries. For example, there are oil and gas funds, precious metals funds and even funds that specialize in industries located in the sun-belt. Today there seems to be a sector fund for every need.

5. **Specialty funds** specialize in specific market sectors such as large-, mid- or small-cap funds, international funds, aggressive growth funds or the now very popular index funds.

6. **Asset Allocation** funds mitigate risk by purchasing stocks and other financial assets such as bonds. For instance, a balanced fund may have 60% of its portfolio in stocks and 40% of its holdings in corporate bonds.

The theory is that in bull markets these funds will not perform as well as pure stock funds, but in bear markets they will not lose as much of their value.

MUTUAL FUND COMMISSIONS

When discussing commissions, mutual funds generally fall into one of two categories: they are either loaded funds or no-load funds.

Both load and no-load mutual funds charge annual management fees. However, loaded mutual funds charge a commission that can be in excess of 5% of the purchase price and may charge ongoing additional fees, such as 12b-1 fees, which can substantially reduce the yield on your investment. No-load funds charge no commissions or 12b-1 fees. So, before buying a mutual fund, it is important to investigate its commissions and fees. Based on every objective article I have read, as well as the performance statistics I have seen, you are better off purchasing no-load mutual funds.

MUTUAL FUND DISTRIBUTIONS

Mutual funds usually allow you to receive interest and dividend payments either monthly, quarterly, semi-annually, etc., or to have them automatically reinvested in your account. Whether you elect to receive your interest, dividends and capital gains or to reinvest them, remember that these distributions are taxable income to you at the end of each year. All funds are required by law to provide you with the distribution information necessary to prepare your individual income tax returns.

MUTUAL FUND MONITORING

Mutual fund results are published daily in most newspapers.

Many financial magazines such as *Money Magazine, Kiplinger's Magazine, Smart Money* and *Forbes* have annual issues that rate mutual funds based on several criteria. Another excellent resource which rates several hundred mutual funds and provides a wealth of information on each fund is the Morningstar Mutual Funds organization (800-876-5005). Finally, one of the best books on mutual funds is *Bogle on Mutual Funds* published by Irwin. John Bogle is the founder of The Vanguard Group which is one of the finest no-load mutual fund companies in the world and his book *tells it like it is.*

If you are going to invest in a mutual fund, I would look for a no-load fund that has proven itself over a period of time (at least five years). You can obtain performance records by requesting prospectuses from the various mutual funds you are interested in or by obtaining information from one of the sources listed above.

Keep in mind that while many mutual funds have excellent records, there are periods of poor performance. Therefore, you must apply the same rules to mutual funds that you applied to buying stocks. Determine your exact investment needs, thoroughly research specific funds, diversify your portfolio and be a long-term investor.

15

Bonds

Steady and Sure?

I N THIS COUNTRY WE ARE conditioned to become borrowers. The danger of easy credit is that it has caused us to focus on *the loan*. Therefore, we've become conditioned to ask questions such as, "which credit card charges us the lowest interest rate (and offers frequent flyer miles)? Where can we obtain the cheapest automobile loan? Where do I get a first mortgage, a second and maybe a third?" All of this in spite of scripture's warning to us:

> *"The rich rule over the poor,*
> *and the borrower is servant to the lender."*
> ***(Proverbs 22:7)***

There is another way. Prudent stewards who have money to invest can become *lenders* instead of *borrowers*, the head instead of the tail.

One of the most efficient and secure methods of becoming a lender is by investing in bonds. *Bonds* are promissory notes between a lender (in this case you) and the borrower (referred to as the issuer) usually a corporation, a government or a governmental agency. The promissory note explains when the issuer will repay the original principal borrowed from the lender. It also explains, in detail, when and how much interest will be paid to the lender until the loan is repaid in full.

The purpose of this chapter is to discuss the various types of bonds available to the astute investor.

CORPORATE BONDS

Corporations raise capital in one of two ways. The first method of raising capital is to sell stock as discussed in the last chapter. A second method of raising capital is for a corporation to borrow money by issuing bonds.

Corporate bonds are binding contracts between an issuer (the corporation) and a lender (you). While it is not the purpose of this chapter to compare the relative merits of stocks and bonds, you should be aware of a basic difference. Stockholders own a fractional interest in a corporation and share in the ongoing successes and/or failures of that company. Stockholders assume more risk in hopes of a greater reward.

Bondholders do not own an interest in the company that they are lending to, however, they generally have the advantage of preferential access to the assets of a company should it go bankrupt. This is due to the fact that a corporation usually pledges its assets as collateral for the bonds it issues. Bondholders receive interest; they do not share in any dividends paid by the corporation or in the increased value of a company's stock.

Bonds contain several basic elements that you should be familiar with.

1. **Name** — All bonds have a legal name by which they are identified and they are issued in $1,000 increments.

2. **Issue Date** — The date the bond was originally offered for sale. The issue date distinguishes a company's bonds from each other.

3. **Maturity Date** — The date the contract ends. At this time the issuer agrees to pay back the face value of the bond to the lender. Maturity dates can range from one to thirty years.

4. **Interest Dates** — The dates that interest is due to the lender or holder of the bond. For example, most bonds will pay interest twice annually at six-month intervals.

5. **Interest Rate** — The rate of interest that each bond pays. This interest rate is expressed as an annual percentage rate and usually does not fluctuate during the life of the bond.

6. **Put and Call Provisions** — With the wild fluctuations in interest rates over the last 15 years, lenders and investors have caused certain provisions to be written into some bond issues:

    a. A **CALL** provision allows the issuer to buy back the bond (redeem it) before maturity at a specific price. This usually happens when interest rates drop and money is now available to the issuer at a lower rate. To offer some protection to the bondholder, certain bonds guarantee a minimum protection time during which the bond cannot be called.

    b. A **PUT** is the opposite of a call. To protect the lender against rising interest rates which would diminish the value of his bond, a put provision allows him to redeem his bond at specified times at the face value of the bond (par).

It is important to understand the put and call provisions, if any, of the bonds you are considering purchasing.

Quality bonds can be very good investments if you understand the relationship between interest rates and bond prices, referred to as *interest rate sensitivity*. **If you don't understand interest rate sensitivity, don't buy bonds.**

An example of interest rate sensitivity is as follows. You purchase a newly issued AT&T bond in the year 2000 with an interest rate of 6%, maturing in 2020. In essence, you have loaned $1,000 to AT&T and received in return a bond which yields 6% and matures in 20 years. AT&T is now legally obligated to pay you 6% interest on your investment for 20 years and then to return your original $1,000 investment to you when the bond matures in the year 2020.

This is all fine, but what if you need your money back before 20 years? This is where the secondary bond market comes into play. This market exists to buy and sell bonds that have already been issued, but have not yet matured. The potential problem is that the resale price of your bond will fluctuate depending on how its original interest rate compares to the current interest rate on newly issued bonds.

Let's suppose two years after you bought your AT&T bond you need to sell it. AT&T is now issuing new $1,000 bonds with a current interest rate of 8%. No one is going to pay you $1,000 for your 6% bond if they can purchase a new bond paying 8%. Therefore, the value of your bond is reduced or "discounted" to make its effective rate equal to an 8% yield. In other words, the bond you paid $1,000 for may now sell for $800 on the secondary bond market. If the value of your bond is discounted, you are faced with the decision of either selling your bond at a loss, holding it for 18 more years until it matures (at which time AT&T will return your $1,000) or waiting and hoping that interest rates will go back down to 6%.

The opposite is also true. If interest rates drop to 5% after you had purchased the 6% AT&T bond, its value would increase. This increase in value is called a "bond premium."

Do not buy bonds until you thoroughly understand how fluctuating interest rates effect the value of issued bonds. Once you understand this principal, you will find that bonds can be excellent investments for a variety of financial objectives.

Now, let's analyze bond investments in terms of safety, liquidity and yield.

SAFETY — Bonds are only as safe as the corporation issuing them is financially secure. Some bonds offer specific collateral as security; others rely on the strength of the issuer to imply safety, government bonds for example. Bonds are rated for safety by two major credit rating companies: Moody's and Standard & Poors. These ratings are:

	Moody's	Standard & Poors
Prime	Aaa	AAA
Excellent	Aa	AA
Good	A	A
Average	Baa	BBB
Fair	Ba	BB
Poor	B	—
Marginal	Caa	B
Default	Ca	D
		C

Bonds used as investments should usually be rated A or better. An occasional Baa/BBB bond may be invested in if you have thoroughly researched the issuer and it appears to be a good investment with a respectable yield. Never invest in a bond rated lower than Baa/BBB; these bonds are considered high-risk/high-yield bonds and are often referred to as junk bonds.

LIQUIDITY — When you purchase a bond, make sure that the initial offering was large enough to establish a secondary trading market. Generally, any bond traded on a major exchange will meet this requirement. A brokerage firm should be able to give you information pertaining to the liquidity of a specific bond issue. Remember, interest rates have a major effect on bond prices in secondary markets. There may be a market available for your bond, but you may receive much less than you paid for it if interest rates have gone up since your purchase.

YIELD — Bond yields are influenced by several factors:
1. Changes in market interest rates (interest rate sensitivity)
2. Issuer (corporate bonds generally pay higher interest rates than comparable U.S. government treasury bonds)
3. Individual bond ratings (AAA bonds will yield less than Baa bonds)
4. Maturity dates (generally the longer the maturity date, the higher the yield)

ZERO COUPON BONDS

Zero coupon bonds are bonds which are sold at deep discounts and redeemed at some point in the future at face value. Zero coupon bonds pay no interest until they mature.

> **EXAMPLE:** AT&T issues a $1,000 zero-coupon bond yielding 12% and maturing in 12 years. You buy that bond for $311.80 today and in 12 years AT&T pays you $1,000. What you have done is locked in 12% interest for 12 years.

Zero coupon bonds have many advantages and disadvantages.

ADVANTAGES

1. Zero coupon bonds allow you to lock in a yield not only on your initial investment, but on the interest on that investment as well. For instance, with a traditional corporate $1,000 bond, you would receive interest semi-annually. However, you may or may not be able to reinvest that interest at 12%. A zero coupon bond automatically reinvests interest payments at the zero coupon bond's interest rate when issued.

2. Zero coupon bonds are excellent vehicles for many investments where taxes are deferred such as IRA's, 401(k) or other pension plans. They are also an excellent way to fund for your children's college education. By purchasing a zero coupon bond for a child, the interest paid may be taxed at the child's lower marginal tax rate.

DISADVANTAGES

1. Yields on zero coupon bonds are harder to calculate. Unscrupulous brokerage firms have been known to charge unusually high commissions on zero coupon bonds, so investigate. Also, due to their popularity, zero

coupon bonds sometimes yield less than similar traditional bonds.

2. Even though you receive no interest from the issuer
   until maturity, the IRS imputes annual interest which
   you must pay income tax on (unless the bond is a zero
   coupon municipal bond).

3. As with traditional corporate bonds, zero coupon bonds
   can have call provisions that in essence defeat the purpose of zero coupon bonds — check it out.

MUNICIPAL BONDS

Municipal bonds are bonds issued by state and local governments
which are tax exempt entities. As such, the interest they pay to you
is not subject to federal income tax nor is it subject to state income
tax in the state of the issuing entity. This tax exemption is the major
difference between corporate bonds and municipal bonds. If you are
in a low tax bracket and the tax exemption is of little value to you,
you are better off with higher yielding corporate bonds. The only
way to know for sure is to consult a chart which compares tax-free
yields to taxable yields at different individual income levels. These
charts are readily available at most book stores or you can call a brokerage firm and they will send one to you.

The following list describes some of the more common types of
municipal bonds.

1. **GENERAL OBLIGATION BONDS** — These bonds
   are issued by a state, city, county or some other taxing
   authority and are backed by that authority's full faith
   and credit as well as its ability to tax.

2. **REVENUE BONDS** — These bonds are issued in
   order to fund a specific project such as the construction

of a building or a bridge and are backed by the revenue generated from the specific project.

3. **HOUSING BONDS** — These bonds are issued to construct a housing project and are backed by the mortgage payments and mortgage insurance, if any, of the project.

SAFETY — Municipal bonds are rated by Moody's and Standard & Poors. You should not buy a municipal bond rated less than A/A. Some bonds have insurance to guarantee interest and or principal repayment. As you would expect, those bonds with high ratings and insurance reduce investor risk and cause yields to drop. As a group, municipal bonds have proven to be extremely safe investments.

LIQUIDITY — With so many municipalities issuing bonds, liquidity is vitally important. Make sure that you purchase issues that have a broad secondary market.

YIELD — Because the yield on municipal bonds is tax exempt, it is always much less than the yield on corporate bonds. Calculate the after tax yield using the tables referred to above. If the after tax yield of corporate bonds is less than the yield on municipal bonds with similar maturity dates, then municipal bonds are probably a good short- to medium-term investment for you.

Municipal bonds are generally best suited for upper income investors. They are not suitable for IRA or any other pension plans as the tax exemption is of no value to these types of investments. Municipal bonds are usually not suitable for children due to their low tax brackets.

BOND FUNDS

A bond fund is a mutual fund comprised of bonds instead of stocks. A mutual fund company will analyze and purchase large quantities of bonds and sell percentage interests to individual investors. Bond funds can hold either corporate or municipal bonds. The funds are generally distinguished by the average maturity of the bonds they hold. For instance, a short-term bond fund's average maturity is 1- 4 years, a medium-term bond fund is 5-10 years and a long-term bond fund will have an average bond maturity of 15-30 years. Generally the bonds purchased are investment grade (BBB) or better.

The advantage of owning a bond fund is diversification. With a bond fund you own a piece of several bonds rather than one or two individual bonds.

Generally, bond funds will be sold in one of two products.

UNIT TRUST — This is a type of closed-end mutual fund. A financial institution will buy a specific number of bonds, put those bonds in a trust and sell units of the trust to the public. The yield is locked in for the duration of the trust, which is when all the bonds mature or are sold. A commission is charged up front, which can be 2-5%. There is no management fee. Risk is limited, yield is good, and liquidity is usually guaranteed by the issuer who will make a secondary market for your units at their underlying value should you desire to sell your units. The resale price of your units will fluctuate with interest rates.

Interest and principal are usually distributed on a monthly basis.

Unit trusts can be short, medium or long term. There are unit trusts of government bonds, corporate bonds, municipal bonds and municipal bonds from specific states.

BOND FUND — A bond fund is an open-ended mutual fund of bonds. In a bond fund, investment grade bonds are constantly being bought and sold to maximize yield. However, you should be aware that the open endedness of bond funds can be a potential problem. The problem being that the bond fund never "matures," that is, there is no specified point in time when you are assured of the return of all of your principal. Interest rate sensitivity can wreak havoc upon the value of bond funds during periods of increasing interest rates. For that reason I generally recommend that investors purchase individual bonds rather than bond funds.

For those who would rather have the diversity and professional management offered by a bond mutual fund, here are some basic rules for purchasing bond funds.

RULES FOR BUYING BOND FUNDS

1. Shop funds. Bond funds can be load or no-load funds. Generally, brokers want to sell loaded funds because the commission is higher. As with all mutual funds, you should compare all commissions and fees before making your purchase. Usually no-load funds are your best bet.

2. In order to determine whether an individual bond fund or a unit trust is best for you, you need to know about how long you intend to own the investment. For example, a unit trust that has a one-time commission charge of 3% is a better deal than a no-load bond fund charging 1/2% a year if you own the unit trust more than 6 years.

3. Explore bond funds for desirable additional services offered such as: automatic reinvestment of interest, insurance on fund assets, the average maturity of the bonds in the fund, and the type of bonds invested in by the fund.

4. Review your funds portfolio via the perspectus. Keep in mind that the lower the ratings of the bonds, the higher the yield and the greater the risk.

U.S. GOVERNMENT BONDS

The U.S. government offers two types of long-term debt instruments: TREASURY NOTES and TREASURY BONDS.

Both types of investments share some common elements:

1. Both Treasury Notes and Treasury Bonds are interest sensitive. This means that their underlying value fluctuates with interest rate fluctuations.

2. Both are backed by the full faith and credit of the U.S. government. This makes the principal as safe as possible and, therefore, sets the base rates by which other investments are compared. For example, an AAA rated corporate bond will usually pay interest approximately 1% higher than the interest rate paid by treasury bonds with similar maturities.

3. Interest paid on treasury obligations is not subject to income tax by state and local governments.

4. In view of the higher interest rates offered by quality corporate bonds, it is probably wiser to buy them rather than treasury obligations. If, however, safety is of the utmost importance to you and yield is a secondary consideration, then treasury obligations are the way to go.

TREASURY NOTES

Treasury notes are issued in face value units of $1,000. They have maturities of between 1 and 10 years and are auctioned at irregular intervals by the Treasury. Since 1983, Treasury notes have been issued in registered form to protect the investor from loss due to stolen or lost notes. Interest is paid by check.

TREASURY BONDS

Treasury bonds are also issued in face value units of $1,000. They have maturities from 5-30 years and can be easily traded on secondary markets.

Because treasury bonds are a long-term security, the underlying value of the bond can change dramatically with fluctuations in interest rates. If you are buying them to accomplish a long-term goal such as providing for the education of your children, they allow you to lock in a good interest rate for a long period of time. However, you are still probably better off buying a AAA or AA rated corporate bond. It is probably just as safe as a treasury note and will pay a higher interest rate. One advantage that a treasury note has over a corporate bond is that the interest paid is not subject to state and local income taxes, but it is still subject to federal income taxation.

16

Gimme Shelter

How to Buy a House

"By wisdom a house is built,
and through understanding it is established;
through knowledge its rooms are filled
with rare and beautiful treasures."
Proverbs 24:3-4

A HOUSE MEANS DIFFERENT THINGS to different people. For some a house is a statement of worth or status, a place to showcase their belongings. For others it is little more than bricks and mortar held together by a monthly mortgage payment. And, for many it represents a place of security and family stability. Whatever the reason, home ownership is a meaningful goal for most of us. In fact, over the next decade more than fifty million families will buy a home. While many people approach the decision to buy a house only from a worldly perspective, as Christians we have an obligation to consider what the Bible says regarding this important subject.

> *"The Lord declares to you that the Lord himself*
> *will establish a house for you:"*
> **(2 Samuel 7:11)**

> *"Unless the Lord builds the house, its builder labors in vain."*
> **(Psalms 127:1)**

> *"The Lord's curse is on the house of the wicked,*
> *but he blesses the home of the righteous."*
> **(Proverbs 3:33)**

In these scriptures we see that a house is a gift from God. It is a temporary dwelling place away from heaven, a momentary shelter to be used as a light to a lost and dying world.

> *"Today salvation has come to this house ... for the Son of Man*
> *has come to seek and to save what was lost."*
> **(Luke 19:9-10)**

When we comprehend this eternal purpose for our home, we can rest in the comfort of His promise in **Psalm 91:1**.

> *"He who dwells in the shelter of the Most High*
> *will rest in the shadow of the Almighty."*

So, include Him in making this important decision.

30 YEARS AND IT'S ALL YOURS

Buying a house can be one of the most exciting and frightening events of your life. There are so many questions racing through your head and just as one is answered, you think of two more.

Let's start at the beginning with that all important first question, "should you really buy a house?" And, the answer for most people is ... probably. Real estate should be one of your portions of eight, and for most families the real estate they invest in is usually their home. If you're young with a growing family, your finances are sound and you plan to live in one place for at least five years, then a house will probably be a good investment for you. However, don't buy a home for the wrong reasons. Don't buy a home solely because you think that it will be a good tax shelter or because it's a "necessary" part of your investment portfolio. Tax laws change and real estate values go through cycles when they are not such a great investment. The primary reason for buying a home should be that the Lord has put that desire in your heart.

Start with prayer. Seek confirmation that He wants you to purchase a home at this particular point in time and then ask for His guidance as you work through the following steps to home ownership:

1. Determining how much house you need
2. Determining how much house you can afford
3. Choosing a location
4. Selecting a real estate agent
5. Negotiating a contract with the seller
6. Finding a lender
7. Closing the deal

1. DETERMINING HOW MUCH HOUSE YOU NEED

When you are sitting in a small apartment and music from your neighbor's stereo pierces through the paper thin walls causing your six-month-old baby who just fell asleep to start crying, any house, anywhere, may seem like a great idea. But, slow down, buying a house will probably be the most expensive purchase you ever make, so it warrants a considerable amount of research, knowledge, wisdom and prayer.

Determining how much house you need begins with the *dream list*.

The dream list describes your perfect house in great detail. It is a list, thoughtfully compiled over a period of time, that contains all of your housing *needs* and *wants*.

Begin your list by describing the location and neighborhood you would like to live in. Next, focus on the house itself. Describe the yard and the exterior features of the home that you desire. Now, move inside and think about the perfect floor plan for your dream home. List all of the rooms that you would like the house to have and the special amenities that you desire for each room. Once you and your spouse are in general agreement over the dream list, put it on your kitchen table and pray over it.

As you search for your dream house you will find that needs and wants will become prioritized based on what you can afford. You may find that a fourth bedroom is more important to you than a big back yard or that you are willing to buy a "fixer upper" and repair it yourself in order to get a more favorable location. Ultimately, with patience, you will find the home that is a good combination of your needs and wants at a price that you can afford.

2. DETERMINING HOW MUCH HOUSE YOU CAN AFFORD

There are formulas that mortgage companies, banks, and savings and loan institutions use as a guide when considering making a home loan to you. Generally, a lending institution will approve a conventional mortgage loan where the total monthly payment for loan principal and interest, property taxes and homeowners insurance does not exceed:

A. 28% of your gross income and/or

B. All of your debts, including your mortgage, do not exceed 36% of your gross income.

These parameters are accepted nationwide, however, I consider them a little aggressive. Personally, I do not like to see anyone commit more than 20% to 25% of their gross income to their mortgage. You are going to be paying on a mortgage for a long, long time, so prayerfully consider what a comfortable monthly payment is for you and your family.

Even more disturbing to me is the current trend of lenders making oppressive loans to families in the form of second mortgages, home improvement loans and debt consolidation loans. Let's review basics. We are stewards. When the Lord entrusts a house to us, good stewardship is not excessively mortgaging that house in an attempt to fund a lifestyle we cannot afford.

There are some other factors you should consider when determining how much to borrow.

- Remember that mortgage interest and real estate taxes are currently deductible on your federal income tax return. You should therefore calculate how much additional cash will be available to you each month since the amount of income tax withheld from your paycheck can now be reduced to reflect the tax savings associated with home ownership.

- Also consider future income. If you are upwardly mobile with a bright future and increases in salary are fairly certain — it's permissible to stretch a little. If on the other hand you're on a fixed income, calculate carefully how much mortgage you can afford so as not to put yourself in a financial bind.

Illustration 9 is a work sheet that will help you determine exactly how much house you can afford.

3. CHOOSING A LOCATION

Location is an important consideration when selecting a new home. The truth is that you are not just buying a new home, you are buying into everything that surrounds that home. If you have any doubt about the validity of this statement, consider the story of Lot as he was choosing a place to live,

> *"Lot looked up and saw that the whole plain of the Jordan was well watered, like the garden of the Lord, like the land of Egypt, toward Zoar ... So Lot chose for himself the whole plain of the Jordan and set out toward the east. The two men parted company: Abram lived in the land of Canaan, while Lot lived among the cities of the plain and pitched his tents near Sodom. Now the men of Sodom were wicked and were sinning greatly against the Lord."*
> ***(Genesis 13:10-13)***

You already know the rest of the story.

Lot's haste to obtain what appeared right for him nearly cost him everything that he possessed including his life. While your decision to purchase a home will probably not be as weighty as Lot's, the point is clear. Wisdom is assessing your home in terms of the surrounding neighborhood and its overall location.

HOME AFFORDABILITY TESTS
SAMPLE PROBLEM

	SAMPLE WORKSHEET	YOUR WORKSHEET
TEST #1 — THE 28% OF GROSS INCOME TEST		
a. What is your gross annual income?	$50,000	
b. Multiply line a by 28%	0.28	0.28
c. Tentative amount available for **mortgage interest, principal, insurance & taxes**	**$14,000**	
d. Divide by 12 for **monthly mortgage payment**	**$1,167**	
TEST #2 — THE 36% OF DEBT TEST		
a. What is your monthly gross income?	$4,167.00	
b. Multiply line a by 36%	0.36	0.36
c. Amount available for debt payments	$1,500	
d. Subtract current monthly debt payments:		
Credit cards	-200	
Auto loan	-350	
Consolidation loan	-175	
e. Tentative amount available for **mortgage interest, principal, insurance & taxes**	**$775**	
MORTGAGE PAYMENT = THE LESSER AMOUNT OF TESTS 1 & 2	**$775**	

ILLUSTRATION 9

Look at the home you are considering buying in terms of its proximity to:

1. The church you will attend
2. Schools and parks
3. Where you work
4. Shopping centers
5. Public transportation
6. Medical facilities
7. Fire, police and emergency units
8. Airports
9. Major highways, access roads and traffic conditions
10. Landfills, flood zones and other undesirable or hazardous areas

Also consider:

11. Are homes in the neighborhood going up or down in value?
12. What are the surrounding neighborhoods like?
13. Is there protective zoning which will guard the value of your property?
14. What is the crime rate like? Inquire for statistics at the local police department.

Finally, drive around without a real estate agent initially. Get the feel of neighborhoods, get out and talk to people working in their yards, ask questions, then narrow your search down to a few areas you consider prime. Do your own leg work, and do it thoroughly — this is where you and your family will live for a long time. Don't rush this decision.

4. SELECTING A REAL ESTATE AGENT

Now it's time to start looking at specific houses and probably the best way to do that is with a real estate agent. Most people don't realize that there are two kinds of real estate agents. The traditional real estate agent is a *seller's agent*, that is, while you may think that the traditional real estate agent represents you, in reality they are paid by the seller and therefore, they actually represent the seller. I wouldn't worry about this too much as the law and the Realtor's Code of Ethics requires that you receive full disclosure on a variety of important subjects including representation. Although you may think that the traditional agent showing you a home is "your agent," that agent has certain legal responsibilities to the seller.

The second type of real estate agent is a buyer's agent. A buyer's agent represents only you, the buyer. Prior to beginning that representation, you will be required to enter into a contract with the buyer's agent. Be careful. Buyer's agents are a relatively new concept and the contract they ask you to sign may have several parts to it with which you are unfamiliar. Have your attorney review and fully explain a buyer's agent's contract to you before you sign it.

Take your time before selecting any real estate agent. Ask your friends who they used as a real estate agent and if they were pleased with the job that the agent did for them. Interview two or three agents and select the one that you think you can work with best. Don't be afraid to check their credentials or to ask them for references. Check out the references they give you. It might also be helpful to inquire about the following:

1. Make sure your agent is qualified through membership in the National Association of Realtors. Membership in this organization requires a certain level of training as well as adherence to a strict Code of Ethics.

2. Ask a potential agent if they specialize in a particular geographic area. In large cities it is impossible for agents to really "know" the entire city. Find an agent who is very familiar with the areas you are interested in.

3. Ask the agent how much help he will give you in finding a lending institution, in helping you understand your financing options and with preparing loan applications.

Finally,

4. Don't let anyone pressure you. If a real estate agent tells you that you'd better make an offer on a house because someone else is interested in the property, let that someone else have it. God will guide you to the house He has for you.

5. NEGOTIATING A CONTRACT WITH THE SELLER

Once you have found your dream house and have decided that it is within your budget, the next step is to make a written offer to the seller. At this stage you should consider retaining an attorney to help you. I realize that an attorney adds extra costs at a time when you need every penny for a down payment, however, this may be the largest purchase you ever make and you may live in this house for decades, so professional help at this point is well worth the extra expense of a good real estate attorney.

Purchase Agreements are several pages long and very complex. At a very minimum the offer will specify particulars of the agreement such as:

- The selling price
- The down payment
- Financing requirements and contingencies

- Appraisal requirements
- A description of exactly what is being sold (including personal property such as appliances and drapes) and what the seller intends to keep (i.e., special chandelier)
- In detail who pays what closing costs
- What repairs are to be made prior to sale
- The requirement that certain inspections (such as roof or termite, etc.) must be passed prior to the act of sale and/or it may require that the seller provide the buyer with a home owners warranty at the closing
- A final inspection date just prior to closing
- A closing date for the transaction to take place

As you can see, the offer to purchase is a complicated contract with a myriad of details that must be considered. Remember everything is negotiable; it is not uncommon for offers to be countered back and forth until a final agreement is finally reached. Be patient, don't lose faith and *put everything in writing*.

6. FINDING A LENDER AND CLOSING THE TRANSACTION

Shopping for financing should be done simultaneously with the search for your home. Start with the financial section of the Sunday newspaper. Most lending institutions will advertise their current mortgage rates and terms in the Sunday paper.

After narrowing your choice down to two or three lending institutions make an appointment with each loan officer to discuss your plans to buy a house. Most loan officers will be happy to explain to you the types of mortgages they offer, the closing costs you should expect to pay and how they calculate the amount of the loan for which you will qualify. Many lending institutions will pre-qualify you for loans up to a specific amount and lock-in an interest rate for you for a specific period of time, such as 30 to 60 days.

> **TYPES OF MORTGAGES** — There are two basic types of mortgages. The first type is the traditional fixed rate mortgage, where the interest rate you pay remains constant throughout the term of the loan. The second type is the floating or adjustable rate mortgage (ARM). In this type of arrangement the interest rate you pay floats based on certain indices. For instance, your mortgage rate may be based on the one-year treasury bill yield plus 3% adjusted every six months. With adjustable rate mortgages it is very important that you **READ THE FINE PRINT.** Innovative lending institutions have developed a variety of ARMs with no two being exactly the same. Make sure you understand the details of the ARM you are considering; if you don't, have your lawyer go over the terms of the loan with you.

Generally, a fixed mortgage allows you to lock-in a fixed interest rate and a level monthly payment for the term of the loan. This can be a wonderful feeling when you have locked in a 6% mortgage rate and current mortgage rates are 10%.

On the other hand, ARMs often allow you to pay less initially and to purchase more home. The risk, of course, is your exposure if interest rates rise significantly. If interest rates rise rapidly the reasonable mortgage payment you now have may increase to the point of causing you financial strain. In order to limit this exposure many lending institutions offers caps or ceilings on their ARMs which specify how much your interest rate can be increased in one year and what the maximum rate can be during the term of the loan. These are important details to investigate if you are considering an

ARM. Some ARMs allow you to convert (usually for a fee) to a fixed rate mortgage after a specified period of time.

7. CLOSING THE DEAL

CLOSING COSTS — No matter what type of mortgage you choose, the buyer will usually incur some closing costs. Closing costs are an assortment of fees and expenses that you pay at the act of sale (or closing). Closing costs can be as much as three to six percent of the loan amount. Lenders are required to give you a good faith estimate of closing costs when you apply for a loan.

The most common closing costs you will encounter are as follows:

> **POINTS** — Points are additional, up-front interest. One point (sometimes called a discount point) equals one percent of the loan you are making. For instance if you are borrowing $80,000 and the loan requires two points, you will have to pay $1,600 in points at the act of sale. When comparing mortgage interest rates it is important to compare the rate offered plus all associated costs, especially points. The best way to do this is by comparing annual percentage rates (APRs). The APR is the true interest rate charged on a loan taking into consideration all additional costs such as points. All lending institutions are required by law to disclose the APR on all loans offered.

> **ORIGINATION FEES** — These fees are another closing expense whose sole purpose is to increase the lending institution's profit at your expense. Origination fees are also calculated as a percentage of the loan amount. When money is tight and mortgage loans are hard to find, origination fees are higher. When money for mortgage loans is in great supply and lending institutions are

competing with one another to make loans, origination fees are low or nonexistent.

REAL ESTATE TAXES AND HOMEOWNER'S INSURANCE — At act of sale you are usually required to have prepaid one year's homeowner's insurance plus the current year's real estate taxes. Subsequent to act of sale, your monthly mortgage payment will include 1/12 of the estimated annual cost homeowner's insurance and property taxes. Your lending institution will deposit these funds into an escrow account each month and then pay the property taxes and homeowner's insurance invoices on your behalf. They do this to protect their interest in your home.

REAL ESTATE COMMISSION — Real estate commission is the fee paid to both the buyer's and the seller's real estate agents. The fee is usually six percent but can be negotiated. The fee is usually paid by the seller, however, typically the seller has built the fee into the asking price of the home.

MISCELLANEOUS CLOSING COSTS — Surveys, appraisals, credit reports, title recordation, title search and an attorney's closing fees are normal closing costs. Estimates of each are required by law to be given to you prior to closing.

TITLE INSURANCE — Title insurance protects you against a loss due to a defect in the title on the property you buy. It is very unlikely that someone could sell you a piece of property that they did not have clear title to, but it happens. Lending institutions will therefore require that you carry enough title insurance to cover the amount of your loan with them. You can also purchase title insurance to cover your down payment. Title insurance is a one-time charge based on the coverage being purchased. It is probably worth the cost just for the peace of mind it buys. Check the policy you are considering purchasing for exclusions.

PRIVATE MORTGAGE INSURANCE — Private mortgage insurance is required by the lender when your down payment is less than 20% of the cost of the house you are buying. Its purpose is to protect the lender in case you default on your mortgage. Private mortgage insurance is paid by the buyer and is calculated at a percentage of the loan.

You now know the basics of buying a house from start to finish. If you are considering buying a house soon, seek the Lord's approval and guidance and then apply what you have learned in this chapter. You should have no problem finding the house God has for you.

17

Ralph

Insurance for Eternity

I T NEVER FAILS TO AMAZE ME that whatever the predicament, the answer can always be found in the Bible. Recently, this was no exception. God was tapping on my shoulder.

Now, I don't mean that He was gently tapping and whispering, "Bob, you're such a great son." No, this was more like the firm hand of a father instructing his son on an important matter. But, the son was very reluctant to listen.

I'd known Ralph for almost twenty years and I can't remember him ever having an unkind word to say about anyone. Ralph was short and he was a life insurance agent — two facts, that we, his close friends never grew tired of harassing him about. He would just laugh and bide his time until he could retaliate ...

Like the time he called my office and with his best middle eastern accent convinced me that he was a wealthy business man that needed help managing his millions. I was already mentally spending my fees when I heard the voice on the other end of the line say, "Gotcha."

Or the time I was paying off a Superbowl lunch bet that I had lost to Ralph and he had prearranged for the waitress to bring me a bill for several hundred dollars at the end of the meal. The cornier the gag, the more he loved it, and the deeper his laughter.

To know Ralph was to know one thing above all else. He adored his family. We all secretly wished that we had been one of his kids.

But, today Ralph was in the hospital dying of cancer.

Ralph was Jewish, unsaved, and God was tapping my shoulder.

I had a choice to make.

That's nothing new — the Bible is packed with stories about making choices. Take Jairus.

He had been up all night. His only daughter was dying. I can't imagine a greater sorrow than to kneel helplessly at the bedside of your child as she passes into the night.

Perhaps it was a neighbor who first told Jairus about the healer in town. Or perhaps his wife had heard about the miracles and begged him to go and talk with the stranger.

Jairus had a difficult choice to make. You see he wasn't just another Jewish believer. He was the ruler of the synagogue. His actions would be scrutinized by the entire congregation. There would be talk. His decision to seek out the healer would pit tradition against faith, ritual against relationship. His social standing would hang in a delicate balance between miracle and mocking.

Bickering voices must have battered his weary mind. "Cling to the comfort of what you know ... no, no, step out in faith, don't miss your miracle ... make a choice, Jairus, make a choice ... your daughter is dying."

I suspect that Jairus was driven as much by fear as by faith as he threw himself in desperation at Jesus's feet and pleaded for his daughter's life.

"Please come to my house, my daughter is dying." A simple step of faith born of agony.

And, only a man familiar with intense suffering could have found the simple words that Jesus used to wrap comfort around Jairus's heart:

"Don't be afraid; just believe, and she will be healed."
(Luke 8:50)

I believe at that moment Jairus was reborn and that a spirit of hope washed over him. There was a new boldness in his step as he threw open the door to his home and marched in with Jesus. Together they threw the doubters and the mockers out of Jairus's house and into the street. After hopelessness and unbelief were removed, Jesus's work was easy:

"My child, get up."
(Luke 8:54)

And she did — up into the arms of a faithful loving father.

****

But, God was still tapping on my shoulder. His message very clear, "Your friend is dying and you must witness to him."

"Oh, Lord, can't You send someone else? I'm not good at witnessing. You gave me other gifts. And besides I was born and raised Jewish, and Ralph is Jewish ... and You know how hard it is for Jewish believers to witness to other Jews. Can't You find me a nice Methodist to witness to?"

I didn't hear any laughter coming from the Lord. For a week His words weighed on my shoulders like stone tablets. His message never changed. I was to witness to Ralph.

Finally, on Sunday morning I couldn't bear the weight any longer. I picked up my keys, hung my head and told Jamie I was going to the hospital. She just smiled.

As I pulled into the hospital parking lot, I prayed, "Please Lord go before me and clear the way. Arrange it so that I can speak to Ralph alone."

I walked into Ralph's room and it was packed with people. Maybe this was a sign. Maybe God had changed his mind.

Literally, within two minutes, everyone in the room said goodbye and left. Now, it was just Ralph, his wife and me.

"Bob, I haven't had a shower in two days. Would you mind sitting with Ralph while I go down the hall and take a shower?"

Just me and Ralph.

I looked at my poor friend and the myriad of tubes and wires piercing his body and knew what I had to do. I just didn't know how to do it. I figured when all else fails, be blunt.

I told Ralph about God's plan of salvation through Jesus. I told him how my life had been drastically and eternally changed. I told him that I wanted to see him in heaven. And then I asked him if he wanted to ask Christ into his heart.

"Yes."

Yes? Wait a minute. He was supposed to get angry and reject me. At least he could have had the courtesy to ask me a few of those questions that no one can answer.

Who knew he'd just say, yes? Now what do I do? I hadn't planned ahead. This was like mustering up the courage to ask a girl out, all along expecting the worst. And, then when she says yes, it sure feels great, but you have no idea what to do next.

I lead Ralph through the prayer of salvation. We cried together and I kissed him on the forehead.

Just as we finished, the room filled with people again.

I felt like Moses at the parting of the Red Sea. I walked into the room and the Lord immediately emptied it of people. And, as soon as Ralph was safely across to the other side, the room filled again.

Two weeks later I attended Ralph's funeral.

I looked around the auditorium packed with people whose lives he had touched with his friendship and compassion. We all loved Ralph, the sound of his laughter and even his corny jokes. I mourned, but the weight on my shoulders had been replaced by a peace in my heart.

The life insurance salesman had chosen the best possible life insurance.

Good bye, old friend.

See you soon.

18

Risky Business

How to Buy
Various Types of Insurance

*"The race is not to the swift
or the battle to the strong,
nor does food come to the wise
or wealth to the brilliant
or favor to the learned;
but time and chance happen to them all.
Moreover, no man knows when his hour will come ..."*
(Ecclesiastes 9:11-12)

IT IS VERY SAD, buy very true that these are the days of lawsuits. The number of lawsuits filed in this country has reached epidemic proportions. Many insurance companies are refusing to write certain types of insurance policies. Other policies that were traditionally renewed at reasonable prices are now being renewed with shocking premium increases. It is a problem that will not disappear and one that will ultimately have to be dealt with by our legislative bodies.

So where does that leave us? Somewhere in the middle, caught between the need to purchase certain types of insurance coverage to protect ourselves and not overspending for that protection. In order to do this we need to establish some ground rules.

First, we must understand that the purpose of any insurance is **financial risk protection**. There exists a statistically small chance that we may be involved in a disaster that would cause us serious financial harm. For instance, our house might burn down or we might be in a serious automobile accident. In order to protect ourselves from the financial consequences of these events, we pool our funds, with millions of other individuals with the same concerns, and purchase protection against financial calamity.

There are six types of insurance that you should consider:

1. Life insurance
2. Automobile insurance
3. Homeowners insurance
4. Umbrella liability insurance
5. Disability insurance
6. Health insurance

The remainder of this chapter will discuss the first five of these six insurances. Health insurance is usually provided by an employer, as opposed to you buying it for yourself, therefore, we will not discuss it in this book. A word of caution: a book could be written on any one of these insurances; this chapter serves only to provide you with an overview of each of these important insurance products.

Before buying any of these insurances you should determine your need and research the various policies available. It is extremely important to also research the company offering the various policies. When you file an insurance claim, you want your insurance company right there ready to aid you, not fighting you every step of the way. Several insurance companies present themselves as a trusted best friend in their advertisements, but in reality, when they were needed to pay claims, consumers rated them poorly.

Consumer Reports magazine and a handful of other publications periodically review and rate various types of insurance policies as well as the companies that issue them. These reports are excellent, objective and often surprising. Do your own homework. Don't buy your insurance from Uncle Charlie because he is a nice guy or Joe just because he goes to your church. The companies they work for may not be so nice.

Before we begin to discuss specific types of insurance I would like to address a question that I am often asked, "Is it scriptural to buy insurance — shouldn't we just trust in the Lord?" As you might expect, scripture does not refer to insurance policies. However, we should always read scripture in light of the larger messages being illustrated by the Lord. Without question, one of these messages is stewardship and the importance of seeking Godly wisdom. The Lord tells us repeatedly that everything is His, that every good gift is from above, and that our responsibility is to properly care for what He has temporarily entrusted to us. In short, we are to be wise stewards. A wise steward will use every proper means available to him to protect what has been entrusted to his care, including insurance.

Now, let's take a look at the specific types of insurance that you may need.

1. LIFE INSURANCE

I have no idea why they call it life insurance. It neither insures that you will live nor pays you for doing so. It's death insurance, paying off only in the event that you are cooperative enough to die. Of course the multi-billion dollar life insurance industry would have a much harder time selling their product if they sold it as death insurance.

And make no mistake, *sell* is the name of the game. When you get married, when you buy a home or a car, when you graduate from school or have a child, you can be sure that someone will call you (usually unsolicited) expounding on the virtues of life insurance.

Perhaps more than any other financial asset, life insurance is the most oversold and misunderstood product pushed onto the average consumer. Using well-scripted "fright stories" and a complex jargon, the life insurance industry has done a good job of keeping the public confused and uninformed. As a result, many consumers buy life insurance that is either unnecessary or wrong for their particular needs.

The purpose of the first section of this chapter will be to guide you through a step-by-step process which will enable you to determine how much and what type of life insurance you may need.

Do you have an insurance need?

Let's start with this basic question. Do you need any life insurance at all?

The answer is — maybe ... maybe not. In order to accurately answer this question you need to determine who would be dependent on your continued financial support if you died today.

Chances are, if you are single with no children, you do not need any life insurance with the exception of perhaps a small policy to cover funeral expenses if your estate would not have enough money in it for that purpose.

Life insurance is designed to provide continued financial support for those who depend on you financially. If no one depends on you financially, then despite the barrage of arguments offered by insurance agents, you most likely do not need any life insurance.

Well then, how about marriage? Does that automatically create a need for life insurance?

Even if you are married you still may not need life insurance. If your family consists of just you and your spouse, and both of you have good jobs, there still may not be a need for life insurance. Again, the key concept is *dependency*. If the death of a spouse would put a financial burden on the surviving spouse (for example, continuing to pay off a mortgage) then life insurance may be necessary. If that death would not financially burden the surviving spouse, and there are no children in the marriage, then life insurance is probably not a necessity.

The true need for life insurance usually arises when you have children.

If you determine that you need life insurance, but your finances are limited, insure the primary wage earner first. Then, if funds are available, the secondary wage earner or homemaker may purchase life insurance. Rarely, is life insurance on a child a wise investment for middle income families.

How much insurance do you need?

Ask two life insurance agents this question and you'll probably get three answers.

Insurance companies usually offer snappy little formulas for calculating insurance needs based on salary. Most of these formulas serve only to prod you into buying a great deal of life insurance. I recommend that you and your spouse calculate your own life insurance need before meeting with a life insurance agent. **Illustration 10** will aid you in calculating that need.

What type of insurance do you need?

Now that you have figured out your life insurance needs, you are faced with the most confusing and difficult part of the process — buying the insurance that's best for you and your family. Life insurance comes in two basic forms:

1. Term life insurance
2. Permanent life insurance

1. TERM INSURANCE

Term insurance is life insurance in its purest form, that is, you are paying solely for the cost of life insurance coverage. With term insurance there is no cash value build up (cash surrender value). Term insurance covers you against death for a specified period of time. Policies are usually issued in one year increments which automatically renew as long as you are willing to pay the increased premium each year.

You can purchase term insurance in one of two basic forms. If you want the face value (amount paid upon death) of the policy to remain the same each year, you would buy *"level term insurance."* Since your chances of dying increase each year, the premium for level term insurance increases accordingly each year. Premiums for level term life insurance are usually very reasonable until age 40 and become cost prohibitive by age 65.

HOW MUCH LIFE INSURANCE DO YOU NEED?

	YOUR ESTIMATES	SAMPLE ESTIMATES
1. Annual income objective		$30,000
2. Minus other sources of annual income		
Surviving spouse's salary		$18,000
Investment earnings		820
Social Security		4,000
Pensions, annuities		0
Miscellaneous (rental income, etc.)		0
Total income		22,820
3. Annual income shortfall		7180
(Subtract total of Item 2 from Item 1)		
4. Amount of death benefit needed to generate annual income in Item 3		119,667
(Divide amount in Item 3 by either .06 or .04)		
5. Expenses		
Funeral expenses		
Cost of last hospital stay/illness		
Estate probate cost		10,200
Federal estate taxes		
State inheritance taxes		
Mortgage balance		0
Education fund		44,232
Emergency fund		6,480
Other outstanding debts		5,000
Total Expenses		65,912
6. Preliminary insurance needs		185,579
(Add Total of Items 4 and 5)		
7. Existing assets/other insurance		
Group life insurance through employer		36,000
Personal life insurance coverages		0
Lump-sum pension payable at death		36,200
Cash and savings		3,300
Securities		5,000
IRA and Keough plans		0
Employer savings plan (401(k))		0
Other liquid assets		8,000
Total assets/insurance		88,500
8. Total Life insurance needed		$97,079
(Subtract Item 7 from Item 6)		

ILLUSTRATION 10

If you prefer that your annual premium remain the same you should buy "*decreasing term insurance.*" Decreasing term insurance has a constant annual premium and an annually decreasing value. This type of policy is often used to cover a financial obligation such as a mortgage.

Usually, past age 65, the cost of term insurance is prohibitive and policies are allowed to expire. By that time, however, your children should be educated, your personal financial situation should be in order, and adequate retirement funds should be available, so that your life insurance needs should be virtually non-existent.

Some term policies will allow you to convert to whole life policies at specific times during the life of the policy, if you so desire.

Term insurance policies should be easy to compare. Since term life insurance is pure insurance, all you need to compare is the cost of the policy and the rating of the company that is issuing the policy. However, beware, prices for term insurance can vary considerably from policy to policy. Your best bet is to comparison shop and find the lowest premium policy available from a reputable company licensed to sell insurance in your state.

Employers and/or certain groups that you may be a member of often offer term insurance at very attractive rates. Tax law allows your employer to provide you with up to $50,000 worth of group term insurance. This benefit is tax free to you and the premium paid is deductible as a business expense by your employer.

Despite the arguments of insurance agents, term insurance meets the true needs of most young families. It provides high face value coverage at low rates. In one's "young family" years, coverage is the most important goal of life insurance and despite arguments to the contrary, the best way to achieve this goal is with term insurance. The real reason life insurance agents don't like term insurance is because they receive almost no commission payout from the sale of term insurance policies, whereas the commissions paid to agents on whole life policies can be substantial.

Most experts agree — in almost every case term insurance is your best buy.

2. PERMANENT LIFE INSURANCE

Generally speaking there are two types of permanent life insurance:

1. Whole life
2. Universal life

Whole Life Insurance

In a typical *whole life policy* you pay a level premium for a period of time usually to age 95 to 100, hence for your *whole life*.

Each year part of the premium you pay goes to commissions, part goes to pay policy administrative expenses, part goes to purchase the death benefit (in essence a term policy) and part is invested, at a fixed rate of return, on your behalf. This invested portion is often referred to as the policy's *cash surrender value*.

The premium you pay for a whole life policy remains constant throughout your life and the policy does not have to be renewed. The invested portion or cash surrender value earns a fixed (usually low) rate of return and is available for you to borrow against in accordance with the terms of your policy.

Participating insurance companies, which are owned and controlled by the policyholders, can pay dividends to their policyholders. These dividends are considered a return of premiums paid and therefore are non-taxable. *Nonparticipating* insurance companies are owned by stockholders and do not pay dividends to policyholders.

Universal Life Insurance

The primary difference between whole life and universal life is how the premium is paid. With universal life the premium you pay goes directly into the cash surrender value of the policy. Periodically, the insurance company will deduct its administrative fees and the cost of insurance from the cash account.

However, unlike whole life insurance, with universal life insurance you can vary the amount of the premium you pay as long as you comply with certain minimum payment requirements. In other words, you can pay a large premium one month and then choose to skip several months of payments. But, be careful not to exhaust your cash surrender value which could cancel your policy coverage.

A hybrid form of universal life insurance which you should be familiar with is *variable universal life insurance*. It is identical to universal life insurance with one important exception. The cash surrender value of this policy can be invested in a variety of investment vehicles such as stock and bond mutual funds. The advantage, of course, is a potentially higher return on your investment, however, there is the disadvantage of increased investment risk.

I like to recommend variable universal life insurance to couples with young children because it aids them in meeting two financial goals. First, it provides insurance protection for the children in case the primary wage earner dies prematurely, and second, it offers a respectable long-term investment vehicle with which to fund for your children's education.

Shopping for Life Insurance

It is important to remember that you buy life insurance from a company not from a life insurance agent. By this I mean, agents come and go. Your interest should be in the financial stability of the company, the quality of the policy itself and the company's reputation for paying claims fairly. It may be advisable to hire an attorney or a CPA to help you compare various insurance companies and the policies they offer.

There are several independent corporations that rate life insurance companies. For a small fee you can contact any of the following to obtain their report:

A.M Best: 908-439-2200, www.ambest.com

Duff & Phelps: 312-368-3198, www.dcrco.com

Moody's: 212-553-0300, www.moodys.com

Standard & Poor's: 212-438-7307,
    www.standardandpoors.com

Weiss Research: 800-289-9222, www.weissratings.com

The best way to determine which polices are the most cost effective is to calculate the difference between what you pay and what you get back from the insurance company. One way to accomplish this is through comparing cost indexes. Cost indexes use several factors, such as premiums paid, cash values, and dividends, to provide you with information that you can use to compare policies.

There are two basic cost indexes: the life insurance surrender cost index and the life insurance net payment cost index. Both indexes are available for all life insurance polices, but you may have to specifically ask your life insurance agent for this information. Generally, the policy with the smaller index number is a better buy than a comparable policy with a larger index number.

Finally, if you do not wish to deal with a life insurance agent there are services which will price insurance policies for you such as:

Quotesmith: 800-431-1147, www.quotesmith.com

Insurance Quote Service: 800-972-1104,
    www.iquote.com

For $50 you can also contact **Insurance Information** at 800-472-5800, for preparation of a much broader analysis of your insurance options.

2. AUTOMOBILE INSURANCE

Automobile insurance is primarily purchased to:

A. Provide liability coverage

B. Provide coverage for personal injuries that you and passengers in your car might sustain

C. Provide coverage for physical damage to your auto

A. Liability coverage is the most important of all automobile insurance coverages. It protects you from financial ruin due to a large liability claim being awarded against you. The two basic types of liability coverage are *bodily injury* and *property damage* coverage. Bodily injury coverage is purchased to cover your legal liability for injuring another person as a result of an automobile accident. This coverage is quoted per person/per accident. For instance, if you have a policy that defines your coverage as $100,000/$200,000, that means that your policy will cover the first $100,000 in liability claims per person injured, with a maximum payout of $200,000 per accident.

Property damage covers your legal liability for damages to another's property resulting from an automobile accident. It is quoted in a flat amount such as $10,000 per accident.

B. *No-fault* insurance covers medical expenses, rehabilitation costs and partial loss of salary benefits for you and your passengers regardless of who is at fault in an automobile accident. Some states require that you carry no fault insurance; others do not. States that do not offer no-fault insurance usually offer *extended benefits* insurance which is similar to no-fault insurance.

Uninsured Motorists insurance covers you and passengers in your car against accidental injury or death caused by an uninsured or hit-and-run driver.

C. The two types of insurance coverage available to protect your vehicle are *Collision insurance* and *Comprehensive insurance*. Collision insurance pays you for damage to your auto resulting from a collision, less your deductible. Comprehensive coverage pays for non-collision damages resulting from calamities such as fire, theft, flood, hail, etc.

Since comprehensive and collision insurance are expensive, you should carefully consider the deductible you choose. The higher the *deductible* (that portion of the damages which you must pay), the lower the policy premium. A deductible of $500 or more, if affordable, can save you hundreds of dollars in premiums each year. The premium savings attributable to several accident-free years will be much greater than the higher deductible you might pay should you have an accident.

Discounts — Most insurance companies offer a variety of discounts to eligible drivers. A few of the more common discounts offered are: multi-car discounts, anti-theft device discounts, good-student discounts and driver training discounts for teenagers. Ask your agent to explain to you the various discounts offered for which you may be eligible.

3. HOMEOWNERS INSURANCE

Homeowners insurance provides coverage for damage to your home, personal belongings and personal liability. The most popular types of homeowners insurance are:

Named Perils Policy (called HO-2 policy) — This policy covers only those losses resulting from specifically named perils. If you suffer a loss due to a peril not specifically insured by the policy, you will not be covered and, therefore, must bear the cost of the loss yourself.

All-Risks Policy (HO-3) — This policy covers all perils except those specifically excluded, which are usually earthquake, flood and nuclear accident. This coverage is your best policy and is usually only slightly more expensive than an HO-2 policy.

When reviewing a homeowners policy you need to look closely at the coverage on your personal belongings. The standard policy provides coverage which equals 50% of the amount of the coverage on the home itself. This dollar amount is usually adequate.

However, most policies replace personal belongings at their depreciated value which causes two big problems for the person suffering the loss. First, depreciated value is usually less than 50% of the original cost of the item damaged, which makes it very hard to replace items without having to spend a lot of your own money to make up for the depreciation. The second problem is that most people keep no records of their personal belongings.

Fortunately, there is a remedy for each of these problems. First, more and more insurance companies are now offering *replacement cost homeowners insurance* which will pay the actual cost to replace your destroyed or damaged belongings. The cost of replacement coverage is only a little higher than the cost of depreciated value coverage. Secondly, I strongly recommend that you write down and/or video tape all of your personal belongings and try to keep receipts for the more expensive items. This log should be updated annually and stored in a safe deposit box.

Bear in mind that coverage for certain possessions such as coin collections, furs, jewelry and other specifically named items will be very limited under your general homeowners policy. There is a separate policy available called a *Personal Articles Floater Policy*, which covers specifically named valuables. This policy is expensive, but should be purchased for very valuable items.

The personal liability coverage provided by your homeowners policy offers very little coverage. Therefore, I recommend that a *personal umbrella liability policy* be purchased to supplement the liability coverage on your home and auto.

4. PERSONAL UMBRELLA LIABILITY INSURANCE

This is one of the least expensive and most needed policies today. It covers personal liability claims against you and your family that exceed the coverage of your auto and homeowners insurance policies. Personal umbrella coverage will start where these policies leave off and provide additional liability coverage up to several million dollars.

In these days of multi-million dollar settlements, the $100,000 of liability coverage your auto policy provides or the $25,000 of coverage your homeowners policy provides is not nearly enough coverage. An umbrella policy will extend that coverage up to a million dollars in coverage for as little as $150 a year.

I cannot overemphasize the importance of this coverage for practically everyone.

5. DISABILITY INSURANCE

Disability insurance, or *income replacement insurance*, provides income to you and your family if you become disabled. Statistically, your chances of being disabled are three times greater than your chances of dying prematurely. It is important that you manage the risk of disability through the purchase of a good individual or group disability insurance contract.

When buying disability insurance you should consider the following factors:

Definition of Disability: Initially, most policies consider you disabled if you are unable to carry on your specific occupation. However, after a year or two of being disabled the policy definition may change and you will only be considered disabled if you cannot perform *any* occupation for which you are suited by occupation, training or experience. If you desire a policy that maintains a *your occupation* definition of disability throughout the life of the policy, it will be more expensive.

Waiting Period: Disability policies will pay benefits after an initial waiting period of 30 to 180 days. The longer the waiting period you choose, the less expensive the policy premium. Typically, a 90-day waiting period is reasonable. (*Note: This is why you need an emergency fund that will provide you with living expenses for at least three months.*)

Duration of benefits: Benefit payments can range from five years to life depending on the policy. Life policies are the only ones that I would consider.

Other questions to be considered when shopping for a disability policy:

1. Are guaranteed monthly benefit increases offered at periodic intervals during the life of the policy?

2. What inflation benefit adjustment options are offered?

3. What happens if you return to work on a less than full-time basis? Will pro-rata benefits be paid if you go back to work part-time?

4. Can the policy be canceled?

5. Are there any standard exclusions, such as pregnancy?

6. Is total disability required to receive a benefit?

7. How are benefits calculated?

8. How difficult is it to file claims, and where are they processed?

9. Is vocational rehabilitation offered?

10. Are premiums waived during the period of disability?

Individual disability insurance policies are expensive. Group policies are generally less expensive, but they do not provide the quality of coverage that the more expensive individually written policies do. In order to have adequate disability coverage, a good compromise is to meet part of your need with the less expensive group policy and then supplement it with an individual policy.

The Author would like to once again thank USAA Educational Foundation for granting him permission to excerpt from their excellent series of financial planning booklets

19

School Days

The High Cost of Higher Education

IT IS COMMON FOR MIDDLE-AGED COUPLES to come into my office with stunned looks on their faces. Finally, mustering up the strength for words, they begin, "I have two children in college and a third who will be entering college in the fall." Pausing, they give me the "as if that's not bad enough" look, and add, "The middle child wants a doctorate in fine arts." Finally, they murmur, "What can we do?"

During the 1980s the cost of college tuition, room, and board grew at twice the rate of inflation. In 1999, this translated into an average annual cost of over $11,000 for state schools and more than $23,000 for private schools. There is no end in sight to these soaring costs. Predictions call for continued increases of approximately 5% a year for the next 20 years. Not a pretty picture.

If you wait until your children are teenagers to begin to fund for their higher education, there is little you can do. Often, you will be faced with the unpleasant choice of having to borrow money, place a second mortgage on your home, or dip into funds intended for retirement.

My best advice is to begin saving for your child's education as soon as you hear "It's a boy" or "It's a girl." The wonder of compound interest is once again the reason for this advice.

How much do you need to save? **Illustration 11** consists of an excellent worksheet and tables that you can use to project future education costs. By completing these forms, you will be able to determine how much you will need to save for each child's education and how much per month it will cost.

In whose name should the funds be accumulated?

There are three basic methods available to you for accumulating an education fund:

1. *The Uniform Gift to Minors Act* (UGMA): One of the most popular ways to shift income is to open an account under the UGMA. UGMA is recognized in all 50 states and allows you to open an account in your child's name and Social Security Number in any bank, homestead, mutual fund, or financial institution. A custodian, usually a parent, is responsible for the account until the child is no longer a minor. You can contribute up to $10,000 per parent per child into these accounts without any gift tax consequences. The income earned in the account for the year 2000 is taxed as follows: there is no federal tax on the first $700 of income, a 15% federal tax is applied to the next $700 of income, and all income over $1,400

is taxed at the parent's income tax rate until the child reaches age 14. These rates are adjusted annually. The major disadvantage of UGMA accounts is that, once the child reaches the age of majority, he or she can legally take the money and spend it on anything.

2. *Educational trusts:* Trust laws vary from state to state, so you will need to discuss specifics with an attorney who specializes in trusts. In general, an educational trust allows for control of the funds by a trustee even when the child reaches the age of majority. In most instances, an independent trustee must be appointed to administer the trust. All gifts to the trust are irrevocable. Educational trusts are probably most appropriate if you intend to accumulate large sums of money for your heirs.

3. *Educational fund in the parent's name:* This method affords you the most control because the assets in the fund stay in your name. In my opinion, the taxes saved by using UGMA accounts or trusts are not enough to risk losing control of the funds. My advice is to establish an educational fund in your name and Social Security Number and to fund it monthly or quarterly.

How should I invest the fund?

Like your retirement funds, these educational funds should be viewed as long-term, conservative investments. The best investment approach is a diversified portfolio of highly rated, no-load equity and bond mutual funds. When your children are young, the portfolio should be substantially invested in equities. As your children approach college age, more of the investment portfolio should be shifted from equities to less risky fixed income investments.

HOW MUCH DO YOU NEED TO SAVE?

Use this worksheet to estimate how much college will cost for your child. You can then calculate how much you will need to invest to reach that goal. The calculations on this work sheet are based on the assumption that college costs will rise 7 percent yearly, a reasonable assumption according to financial planning experts. Fill out the form below using using Table A and Table B on the next page to assist you in determining your monthly savings amount.

	Your Estimate	Sample Estimate
1. Years in college: You may give yourself more time by using child's senior college year as your target date		16
2. Current annual cost of tuition, fees, room and board:		$8,500
3. College cost inflation: See Table A to find the inflation factor to use given your time horizon		2.95
4. Future annual college cost: Multiply #2 by #3		$25,075
5. Future total college cost: Multiply #4 by number of years you expect child will attend college		$100,300
6. After-tax rate of return factor: See Table B to find the appropriate return factor. Look under your anticipated rate of return and opposite the years remaining to college		27.89
7. Annual savings amount required: Divide #5 by #6.		$3,596
8. Monthly savings amount required: Divide #7 by 12		$299

* Two references available through high school guidance counselors provide good average cost figures. They are the College Board's *College Cost Book* and the ACT's *College Planning/Search Book*. For 1997-1998, the average annual cost of tuition, room and board at a public school was $10,069 and a private school was $21,424.

ILLUSTRATION 11

(Illustration 11 is copied with the permission of The USAA Educational Foundation. Permission to reprint does not constitute a third-party endorsement of products, services or publications. Any other usage of this material is expressly prohibited without the permission of The USAA Educational Foundation.)

TABLE A

Years To College	Inflation Factor
1	1.07
2	1.15
3	1.23
4	1.31
5	1.40
6	1.50
7	1.61
8	1.72
9	1.84
10	1.97
11	2.10
12	2.25
13	2.41
14	2.58
15	2.76
16	2.95
17	3.16
18	3.38
19	3.62
20	3.97
21	4.14

TABLE B

Years To College	3%	4%	5%	6%	7%	8%	9%
1	1.00	1.00	1.00	1.00	1.00	1.00	1.00
2	2.03	2.04	2.05	2.06	2.07	2.08	2.09
3	3.09	3.12	3.15	3.18	3.22	3.25	3.28
4	4.19	4.25	4.31	4.38	4.44	4.51	4.57
5	5.31	5.42	5.53	5.64	5.75	5.87	5.99
6	6.47	6.63	6.80	6.98	7.15	7.34	7.52
7	7.66	7.90	8.14	8.39	8.65	8.92	9.20
8	8.89	9.21	9.55	9.90	10.26	10.64	11.03
9	10.16	10.58	11.03	11.49	11.98	12.49	13.02
10	11.46	12.01	12.58	13.18	13.82	14.49	15.19
11	12.81	13.49	14.21	14.97	15.78	16.65	17.56
12	14.19	15.03	15.92	16.87	17.89	18.98	20.14
13	15.62	16.63	17.71	18.88	20.14	21.50	22.95
14	17.09	18.29	19.60	21.05	22.55	24.22	26.02
15	18.60	20.02	21.58	23.28	25.13	27.15	29.36
16	20.16	21.83	23.66	25.67	27.89	30.32	33.00
17	21.76	23.70	25.84	28.21	30.84	33.75	36.97
18	23.41	25.65	28.13	30.91	34.00	37.45	41.30
19	25.12	27.67	30.54	33.76	37.38	41.45	46.02
20	26.87	29.78	33.07	36.79	41.00	45.76	51.16
21	28.68	31.07	35.72	39.99	44.97	50.42	56.76

HIGHLIGHTS OF TAX BENEFITS FOR HIGHER EDUCATION

	Hope Credit (Education credit)	**Lifetime Learning credit** (Education credit)	**Eduction IRA[1]**	**Traditional and Roth IRAs[1]**
What is your benefit?[2]	Tax credit (nonrefundable)	Tax credit (nonrefundable)	Withdrawals are tax free	No 10% additional tax on early withdrawal
What is the annual limit?	Up to $1,500 per student	Up to $1,000 per family	$500 contribution per child under 18	Amount of qualifying expenses
What expenses qualify besides tuition and required enrollment fees?[2]	N/A	N/A	Books, supplies, and equipment; room and board if at least half-time attendance; payments to qualified state tuition program	Books, supplies, and equipment; room and board if at least half-time attendance
What education qualifies?	1st 2 years of undergraduate	Applies to expenses paid and to school attendance after June 30, 1998	All undergraduate and graduate levels	All undergraduate and graduate levels
What other conditions apply?	Can be claimed only for 2 years; must be enrolled at least half-time in a degree program		Contributions not deductible; cannot also contribute to qualified state tuition program or claim an education credit; Must withdraw assets at age 30	Must receive entire balance or begin receiving withdrawals by April 1 of following year in which age 70.5 is reached
At what income range do benefits phase out?	$40K – $50K $80 – $100K for joint returns	$40K – $50K $80 – $100K for joint returns	$95K – $110K $150 – $160K for joint returns	N/A

CAUTION: No double benefits are allowed.

ILLUSTRATION 12

HIGHLIGHTS OF TAX BENEFITS FOR HIGHER EDUCATION

	Interest Paid on Student Loans	Qualified State Tuition Programs	Qualified U.S. Savings Bonds[1]	Employer's Education Assistance Program[1]
What is your benefit?	Deduction to arrive at adjusted gross income	Prepay future tuition expenses	Interest is excludable from income	Employer benefits are excludable from income
What is the annual limit?	1998: $1,000 1999: $1,500 2000: $2,000 2001: $2,500	None	Amount of qualifying expenses	$5,250
What expenses qualify besides tuition and required enrollment fees?[2]	Books, supplies, and equipment; room and board; transportation; other necessary expenses	Books, supplies, and equipment; room and board if at least half-time attendance	Payments to qualified state tuition program; payments to education IRAs	Books, supplies, and equipment
What education qualifies?	All undergraduate and graduate levels	All undergraduate and graduate levels	All undergraduate and graduate levels	Undergraduate level
What other conditions apply?	Applies to 1st 60 months' interest; must be enrolled at least half-time in a degree program	Tax deferred earnings are taxed to beneficiary when withdrawn	Applies only to qualified series EE Bonds issued after 1989 or Series I Bonds	Cannot also claim an education credit; expires for courses beginning after May 31, 2000
At what income range do benefits phase out?	$40K – $55K $60K – $75K for joint returns	N/A	1998: $52,250K – $67,250 $78,350K – $108,350K for joint returns	N/A

[1] Any nontaxable withdrawal is limited to the amount that does not exceed qualifying educational expenses.
[2] You must generally reduce qualifying educational expenses by any tax-free income. You generally cannot use the same educational expense for figuring more than one benefit.

Where can I go for information on financial aid?

There are several private and governmental organizations whose sole purpose is to help college bound students obtain financial aid.

The Federal government has an assortment of programs to aid students with the cost of higher education. For their *Student Guide* you can contact the Federal Student Aid Information Center, P.O. Box 84, Washington, D.C. 20044, (800)-433-3243. You can also contact the U.S. Department of Education for additional useful information at *www.fafsa.ed.gov.* Individual states also offer a variety of financial aid packages. Your child's high school guidance counselor should be able to direct you to appropriate state agencies.

Another useful site for obtaining financial aid information is the College Board's web site, *www.collegeboard.org.*

Private sources for financial aid can be researched through The Financial Aid Information Page's website, *www.finaid.org.*

Finally, there are federal government tax incentives available to offset some of the expense of higher education. **Illustration 12** summarizes several of the major tax benefits available for higher education. If you need a more detailed explanation regarding these benefits the IRS offers an excellent booklet entitled Publication 970 Tax Benefits for Higher Education. You can obtain a free copy by calling 800-829-1040.

20

The Gold Watch

Planning for Retirement

WALK INTO ANY BOOKSTORE and go to the financial section. There you will find endless shelves of books espousing two themes: how to get rich and how to retire early.

Now, pick up any Bible and go to the concordance. Look up the word "retire" and you will find nothing ... no mention of retire, retiring, retirement ... nothing. In fact the only story that I can find in the Bible that vaguely relates to retirement is in Luke:

> *"The ground of a certain rich man produced a good crop.*
> *He thought to himself,*
> *'What shall I do? I have no place to store my crops.'*
> *Then he said, 'This is what I'll do. I will tear down my barns*
> *and build bigger ones, and there I will store all my grain and*
> *my goods. And I'll say to myself, You have plenty of good things*

laid up for many years. Take life easy; eat,
drink and be merry.'
But God said to him, 'You fool! This very night
your life will be demanded from you.
Then who will get what you have prepared for yourself?'"
(Luke 12:16-20)

There is no retirement for Christians.

Shocked? Well, understand this statement in its proper context. Scripture says we are bond servants, called to the *great commission,*

"Go into all the world and preach the good news to all creation."
(Mark 16:15)

Nowhere, in all sixty-six books of the Bible, can I find the phrase, "until age 65." Rather, *John 9:4* instructs us:

"As long as it is day, we must do the work of him who sent me.
Night is coming, when no one can work."

That work, until our last breath, is to spread the gospel message. There is no retirement for Christians.

There is, however, a time when most of us will retire from our *secular* jobs. Good stewardship demands that we be financially able to support ourselves when that time comes.

To prepare for this transition we need to ask ourselves a few basic questions.

How Much Will I Need to Retire?

The following chart illustrates how you can expect to fare at retirement based on your pre-retirement income.

PERCENT OF PRE-RETIREMENT INCOME

0%	50%	70%	100%
Trouble	Fair-Good	Excellent	

By reading the chart from left to right you can determine the relative health of your financial situation at retirement. If at retirement your retirement income will be 0 to 50% of what you were earning immediately prior to retirement, you're in for trouble. Chances are you will have to severely cut back your standard of living. If your retirement income will be 50 to 70% of your pre-retirement income, you'll be in the fair to good range. As a rule of thumb, you will want to receive at least 60% of your pre-retirement income at retirement. If your retirement income is 75% or greater of your pre-retirement income, you should be in excellent financial shape throughout your retirement years.

So How Do You Get There?

Your retirement income will generally come from four major sources:

1. Social Security
2. Employer and self-employed retirement plans
3. Individual retirement plans
4. Investment income

For most people, Social Security will provide about 20 to 25% of their retirement income. An additional 30 to 40% of your retirement income will need to come from your retirement plans and a similar percentage from earnings on your investments.

1. SOCIAL SECURITY

We often hear, "I don't know why I have to contribute to Social Security, by the time I'm old enough to collect Social Security the system will be bankrupt!" Probably not. Changed, yes, but bankrupt, I doubt it. "Baby boomers" are getting older, thereby pushing up the average age of the population. This means that more and more people will be collecting Social Security which is a good news/bad news situation.

The good news is that this aging population will be a political force to be reckoned with, and therefore, Social Security will not be abandoned by politicians.

The bad news is that in order to keep Social Security solvent, we can expect a variety of changes to the system, including increasing the age at which you will collect benefits, reducing the amount of benefits paid, capping benefit payments, increasing the taxable Social Security wage base and increasing the amount of benefits that will be subject to income tax. These compromises are fair, if you remember that Social Security was never intended to provide all of your retirement income. Its purpose is to supplement it.

The Social Security system provides benefits to the retiree in two major ways. First, at age 62 a retired worker can elect to begin receiving retirement checks. If you reach age 62 in 2000, your monthly retirement can be as much as $1200. However, you do not have to retire at age 62. For instance, if that same person waited to retire until age 65 his monthly benefit would be 20% higher or approximately $1433; and a married couple could receive a maximum monthly benefit of $2149. The average social security benefit paid today is approximately $780 a month. The actual benefit you will receive depends on your age, how long you have worked, and how much you have contributed to the Social Security system while you were in the workforce.

The second major retirement benefit provided by the social security system is Medicare. Medicare is comprised of two parts: hospital insurance (often referred to as Part A coverage) and medical insurance (referred to as Part B coverage). You must be at least 65 to qualify for Medicare benefits.

The hospital insurance part of Medicare helps pay the cost of inpatient hospital care. The medical insurance part of Medicare helps pay the cost of physicians' services and for certain other medical items and services not covered by hospital insurance. People who have Medicare medical insurance share in the cost of coverage. In 2001, each participant pays approximately $50 a month to have Medicare medical insurance. Medicare insurance covers only about 40% of your actual health care costs. It is important, therefore, to consider purchasing private Medicare Supplemental Insurance (often referred to as "gap" coverage) and Long Term Care insurance.

For more information you can contact the Social Security Administration and Medicare as follows:

Social Security Administration
800-772-1213, www.ssa.gov

Ask for the useful free publications:
Understanding The Benefit and
How Your Retirement Benefit is Figured

You should also request a copy of *Your Social Security Statement*. This helpful report will tell you which benefits you qualify for, when you will receive them, and how much you can expect to receive.

Medicare Hotline
800-638-6833, www.hcfa.gov or www.medicare.gov

Ask for the useful free publications:
The Medicare Handbook and *Medicare,*
Guide to Health Insurance for People with Medicare

2. EMPLOYER AND SELF-EMPLOYED RETIREMENT PLANS

One of the saddest statistics I am aware of is that between eighty and ninety percent of the people who retire in the United States, the wealthiest country in the world, will live solely on their Social Security check. To avoid being part of this unfortunate statistic, you must begin to accumulate retirement funds both individually and through any type of retirement plan that your employer offers, as soon as possible.

Illustration 13 is an excellent spreadsheet which provides you with a wealth of information on the major types of employer and self-employed retirement plans available.

3. INDIVIDUAL RETIREMENT PLANS

The primary retirement account options available to individuals are Individual Retirement Accounts (IRAs). We have already reviewed the Education IRA in **Illustration 12** in Chapter 19. The Traditional IRA and the Roth IRA are two additional options available for most people.

The Traditional IRA allows you to make annual contributions of up to $2,000 which may be tax deductible subject to certain Internal Revenue Service regulations. Income tax is deferred on the growth in a Traditional IRA until you begin to make withdrawals from the account.

Subject to certain eligibility rules a Roth IRA also allows you to contribute up to $2,000 annually. Contributions into a Roth IRA are not deductible. However, once a taxpayer has reached age 59 1/2, distributions from a Roth IRA are not subject to income tax.

As with any type of retirement plan there are many rules and regulations regarding eligibility, deductibility, distributions and tax consequences.

One excellent source of information on retirement planning and retirement plans can be located at the Charles Schwab & Co., Inc. website, *www.schwab.com*. Or you can call Charles Schwab & Co. Inc. at 1-800-435-4000 and request the following excellent publications:

Schwab Smart Retirement Guide

Schwab IRAs

Schwab Custodial IRA

Schwab College Saver Program

Schwab Retirement Solutions for Business

4. INVESTMENT INCOME

Throughout this book we have discussed the goal of increasing our net worth. Here is why. After years of good stewardship we want to have accumulated a solid investment portfolio. Now is the time to put these assets to work for you. Properly managed, they will continue to provide you with supplemental income for the rest of your life, freeing you to accomplish God's plan for your life, unencumbered by financial worry.

All of the lessons of financial stewardship weave together for one ultimate purpose: to be free from financial bondage in order to accomplish the will of the Father and be able to say to him,

> *"I have brought you glory on earth by completing*
> *the work you gave me to do."*
> ***(John 17:4)***

That's it. That is our purpose for being here.

RETIREMENT PLAN COMPENSATION
SEP-IRA *(Simplified Employee Pension)*

Who may use	Corporation, partnership, self-employed, S corporation, nonprofit.
Client profile	Best suited for business owners who want simplicity. Ideally suited for companies with more volatile profits and low employee turnover.
Deadline for establishing	Tax filing due date, including extensions.
Deadline for employer contributions	Due date of employer's tax return, including extensions.
Who must be included	Any employee who is age 21 or older and has worked for the employer for any part of three of the last five plan years. May exclude employees earning less than $450 per year.
Obligation to contribute[1]	Employer makes discretionary contributions and can change or discontinue them each year.
Maximum annual combined contribution from the employer and employee that the employer may deduct	15% of employee's pay (maximum eligible pay per employee is $170,000)
Maximum annual allocation[2] to employee's account	15% of employee's gross pay or $30,000, whichever is less.
Maximum annual employee contribution	No employee contributions allowed, except in grandfathered SAR-SEPS.
Vesting	Immediate 100% vesting.
Reporting and disclosure	When plan has been established, employer fills out SEP agreement and gives a copy to the employee when the employee becomes eligible. No additional annual reporting is required

ILLUSTRATION 13

RETIREMENT PLAN COMPENSATION
Profit Sharing *(Defined Contribution)*

Who may use	Corporation, partnership, self-employed, S corporation, nonprofit.
Client profile	Best suited for companies with more volatile profits where employee turnover may be a problem and the desired contribution rate does not exceed 15% of payroll.
Deadline for establishing	Last day of employer's tax year.
Deadline for employer contributions	Due date of employer's tax return, including extensions.
Who must be included	Any employee who is age 21 or older with 1,000 hours of service in two 12-month periods. Can exclude certain employees.
Obligation to contribute[1]	Unless fixed as a percentage of compensation or profits, contributions are at the discretion of the employer and are not dependent on profits.
Maximum annual combined contribution from the employer and employee that the employer may deduct	15% of total eligible payroll (maximum eligible pay per employee is $170,000).
Maximum annual allocation[2] **to employee's account**	25% of employee's gross pay or $30,000, whichever is less.
Maximum annual employee contribution	No employee contributions allowed.
Vesting	Vesting schedules available when using a maximum of one-year-of-service eligibility requirements.
Reporting and disclosure	Full ERISA requirements. IRS Forms 5500, 5500-C, 5500-R or 5500-EZ and applicable schedules must be filed annually.

ILLUSTRATION 13 (Continued)

RETIREMENT PLAN COMPENSATION
Age-Weighted/Cross-Tested Profit Sharing *(Defined Contribution)*

Who may use	Corporation, partnership, self-employed, S corporation, nonprofit.
Client profile	The **Age-Weighted** profit sharing plan is best suited for companies that want to favor older employees.
	The **Cross-Tested** plan is best suited for companies that want to favor particular groups of employees who are, on average, older employees.
Deadline for establishing	Last day of employer's tax year.
Deadline for employer contributions	Due date of employer's tax return, including extensions.
Who must be included	Any employee who is age 21 or older with 1,000 hours of service in two 12-month periods. Can exclude certain employees.
Obligation to contribute[1]	Unless fixed as a percentage of compensation or profits, contributions are at the discretion of the employer and are not dependent on profits.
Maximum annual combined contribution from the employer and employee that the employer may deduct	15% of total eligible payroll (maximum eligible pay per employee is $170,000).
Maximum annual allocation[2] **to employee's account**	25% of employee's gross pay or $30,000, whichever is less.
Maximum annual employee contribution	No employee contributions allowed.
Vesting	Vesting schedules available when using a maximum of one-year-of-service eligibility requirements.
Reporting and disclosure	Full ERISA requirements. IRS Forms 5500, 5500-C. 5500-R or 5500-EZ and applicable schedules must be filed annually.

ILLUSTRATION 13 (Continued)

RETIREMENT PLAN COMPENSATION
Money Purchase *(Defined Contribution)*

Who may use	Corporation, partnership, self-employed, S corporation, nonprofit.
Client profile	Best suited for companies with stable yearly profits. May be useful in combination with a profit sharing plan, subject to combined limit of lesser of 25% or $30,000 of compensation.
Deadline for establishing	Last day of employer's tax year.
Deadline for employer contributions	Due date of employer's tax return, including extensions.
Who must be included	Any employee who is age 21 or older with 1,000 hours of service in two 12-month periods. Can exclude certain employees.
Obligation to contribute[1]	Employer is required to make contribution as elected in adoption agreement at plan establishment.
Maximum annual combined contribution from the employer and employee that the employer may deduct	25% of employee's eligible pay, up to $30,000 (maximum eligible pay per employee is $170,000).
Maximum annual allocation[2] to employee's account	25% of employee's gross pay or $30,000 whichever is less.
Maximum annual employee contribution	No employee contributions allowed.
Vesting	Vesting schedules available when using a maximum of one-year-of-service eligibility requirements.
Reporting and disclosure	Full ERISA requirements. IRS Forms 5500, 5500-C, 5500-R or 5500-EZ and applicable schedules must be filed annually.

ILLUSTRATION 13 (Continued)

RETIREMENT PLAN COMPENSATION
Defined Benefit Pension Plan *(Defined Benefit)*

Who may use	Corporation, partnership, self-employed, S corporation, nonprofit.
Client profile	Best suited for established companies with consistent profits. Benefits companies with key employees age 50 or older.
Deadline for establishing	Last day of employer's tax year.
Deadline for employer contributions	Due date of employer's tax return, including extensions.
Who must be included	Any employee who is age 21 or older with 1,000 hours of service in two 12-month periods. Can exclude certain employees.
Obligation to contribute[1]	Employer must make contribution dictated by the benefit formula and calculated annually by an actuary.
Maximum annual combined contribution from the employer and employee that the employer may deduct	Contribution is not limited (maximum pay per employee to determine benefits is $170,000). **Note:** Annual benefit from the plan may not exceed the lesser of 100% of participant's compensation or $135,000.
Maximum annual allocation[2] **to employee's account**	No individual accounts.
Maximum annual employee contribution	No employee contributions allowed,
Vesting	Vesting schedules available when using a maximum of one-year-of-service eligibility requirements.
Reporting and disclosure	Full ERISA requirements. IRS Forms 5500, 5500-C, 5500-R or 5500-EZ and applicable schedules must be filed annually.

ILLUSTRATION 13 (Continued)

RETIREMENT PLAN COMPENSATION
SIMPLE-IRA & SIMPLE-401(k) *(Savings Incentive Match Plan for Employees)*

Who may use	Corporation, partnership, self-employed, S corporation, nonprofit and government entities. Business must have 100 or fewer employees and cannot fund any other qualified plan in current year.
Client profile	Best suited for employers who want to encourage employee retirement savings and avoid costly administration. Employer obligation to contribute is relatively small compared with other plan choices.
Deadline for establishing	October 1 for contributions in current calendar year. (Plan year must be calendar.)
Deadline for employer contributions	Due date of employer's tax return, including extensions. Deferrals must be deposited no later than 30 days following month of payroll.
Who must be included	Any employee who earned $5,000 or more during any two preceding years and is expected to earn $5,000 or more in the current year. For SIMPLE-401(k), see 401(k) column.
Obligation to contribute[1]	Employer contribution required. Choice of dollar-for-dollar matching contribution up to 3% of employee's compensation or nonelective, non-matching contribution of 2% of compensation for all eligible employees.
Maximum annual combined contribution from the employer and employee that the employer may deduct	SIMPLE-IRA — $12,000 ($6,000 maximum match up to 3% of pay plus $6,000 deferral). SIMPLE-401(k) — see 401(k) column.
Maximum annual allocation[2] to employee's account	Refer to maximum combined contribution, above.
Maximum annual employee contribution	$6,000 (adjusted for cost-of-living increases).
Vesting	Immediate 100% vesting.
Reporting and disclosure	Minimal for SIMPLE-IRA. Employer must give employees Summary Plan and Contribution Notice no later than November 2 each year. For SIMPLE-401(k), see 401(k) column.

ILLUSTRATION 13 (Continued)

RETIREMENT PLAN COMPENSATION
401(k) Profit Sharing *(Defined Contribution)*

Who may use	Corporation, partnership, self-employed, S corporation, nonprofit (excluding government entities).
Client profile	Best suited for employers that want to minimize employer contributions and encourage employee savings.
Deadline for establishing	Last day of employer's fiscal year, but no later than commencement of employee contributions.[5]
Deadline for employer contributions	Due date of employer's tax return, including extensions. Deferrals must be deposited no later than 15 days following month of payroll.
Who must be included	Any employee who is age 21 or older with 1,000 hours of service within 12 months. Can exclude certain employees.
Obligation to contribute[1]	Contributions come from employee salary reduction and/or from employer. **Safe Harbor:** Requires one of the following employer contributions: • dollar-for-dollar on first 3% deferred; 50 cents on next 2% deferred • non-matching contribution of 3% of compensation for all eligible employees.
Maximum annual combined contribution from the employer and employee that the employer may deduct	15% of total eligible payroll (maximum eligible pay per employee is $170,000).
Maximum annual allocation[2] **to employee's account**	25% of employee's gross pay or $30,000, whichever is less.
Maximum annual employee contribution	Elective contributions up to 25% of net annual compensation,[3] not to exceed $10,500.
Vesting	**Employee elective deferrals:** immediate 100% vesting. **Non-Safe Harbor employer contributions:** Vesting schedules available. **Safe Harbor employer contributions:** immediate 100% vesting.
Reporting and disclosure	Full ERISA requirements. IFIS Forms 5500, 5500-C or 5500-R and applicable schedules must be filed annually. Discrimination test applies to deferrals for Non-Safe Harbor plans.

ILLUSTRATION 13 (Continued)

RETIREMENT PLAN COMPENSATION
403(b)

Who may use	Organizations qualified under IRC section 501(c)(3), such as schools, churches and hospitals.
Client profile	Best suited for employers that want to minimize employer contributions and encourage employee savings, particularly plans that will be employee-funded only.
Deadline for establishing	Can be established any time during calendar year.
Deadline for employer contributions	Due date of employer's tax return, including extensions.
Who must be included	All employees of qualified organizations; some exclusions may be allowed.
Obligation to contribute[1]	Contributions typically come from employee salary reduction. Employer contributions are permitted but may subject the plan to additional reporting/discrimination requirement.
Maximum annual combined contribution from the employer and employee that the employer may deduct	25% of employee's eligible pay up to $30,000 (maximum eligible pay per employee is $170,000).
Maximum annual allocation[2] **to employee's account**	25% of employee's gross pay or $30,000, whichever is less.
Maximum annual employee contribution	Up to 20% of net annual compensation,[3] not to exceed $10,500.[4]
Vesting	**Employee elective deferrals:** immediate 100% vesting. **Employer contributions:** Vesting schedules available.
Reporting and disclosure	If employer makes contributions, IRS Forms 5500, 5500-C or 5500-R must be filed annually.

ILLUSTRATION 13 (Continued)

RETIREMENT PLAN COMPENSATION
457 Plan *(Nonqualified Deferred Compensation)*

Who may use	State and local governments and nonprofit organizations, such as universities and hospitals. Does not include churches and qualified church-controlled organizations.
Client profile	Best suited for employers that want to minimize employer contributions and encourage employee savings.
Deadline for establishing	Due date of employer's tax return, including extensions.
Deadline for employer contributions	Due date of employer's tax return, including extensions.
Who must be included	Any employee who is age 21 or older with 1,000 hours of service within 12 months. Can exclude certain employees.
Obligation to contribute[1]	Employer is not obligated to make contributions. All contributions are voluntary salary reductions.
Maximum annual combined contribution from the employer and employee that the employer may deduct	Employee contributions limited to 33 1/3% of includable compensation with a maximum of $8,000. Employee and employer contributions combined are unlimited.
Maximum annual allocation[2] **to employee's account**	$8,000. A limited catch-up provision can be used for any or all of the last three years before normal retirement age.
Maximum annual employee contribution	$8,000 (adjusted for cost-of-living increases).
Vesting	**Employee elective deferrals:** Immediate 100% vesting. **Employer contributions:** Vesting schedules available.
Reporting and disclosure	Under some circumstances, may require full ERISA reporting

ILLUSTRATION 13 (Continued)

RETIREMENT PLAN COMPENSATION
Ilustration Footnotes

1 Top-heavy minimums apply when more than 60% of account balances accrued benefits are attributable to key employees (or for SEP-IRAs, 60% of aggregate contribution for key employees).
2 Allocation refers to the total of employer-deductible contributions, forfeitures, and any employee salary deferral or voluntary after-tax contribution.
3 Compensation is amounts shown on W-2 (wages, salaries, bonuses, etc.) and self-employed earned income.
4 Maximum exclusions, allowances and/or catch-up options may affect individual deferral limits.
5 Safe Harbor 401 (k) plans must be established before the effective date and must be at least three months long.

ILLUSTRATION 13 (Continued)

(Illustration 13 is reprinted with the permission of A.G. Edwards & Sons, Inc.)

(Portions of this chapter were adapted from Robert Katz, *The Family Practitioner's Survival Guide to the Business of Medicine*, chapter 9, pages 109-114, ©1998, Aspen Publishers, Inc.

21

Reader's Choice

The Eighth Portion

"Give portion to seven, yes to eight,
for you do not know what disaster
may come upon the land."
Ecclesiastes 11:2

RECENTLY I TOOK MY CHILDREN to one of the
new mega-bookstores. While they were roaming the
aisles, browsing from shelf to book-stuffed shelf, I
decided to sit down for a moment in one of the cozy
chairs they provide. As I sat there I noticed a magazine on the table
next to me. I picked it up and was surprised to find that the entire
magazine was dedicated to Beanie Babies®.

And I mean dedicated. There were articles about caring for
Beanie Babies® and how to grade the quality of Beanie Babies®.
There were letters to the editor about Beanie Baby topics I never

dreamed existed. There was an international Beanie Baby page where pen pals from around the world discussed the relative merits of these bean-stuffed pieces of cloth. And, of course, there was a listing of every single Beanie Baby ever manufactured and it's supposed value. Beanie Babies®!

The flesh often desires to give value to the ridiculous, therefore we should heed this warning as we discuss the eighth portion, collectibles: they are not for everyone.

Collectibles are items purchased with the hope that their value will increase over time. The list of what people collect is endless. However, some of the more popular collectibles are items such as:

Art

Coins

Stamps

Antique furniture

Gold and silver

Dolls

Glassware

Antique toys

Old books and manuscripts

Maps

Movie posters

Vintage automobiles and motorcycles

Antique jewelry

Baseball cards

and on, and on, and on.

The popularity of television shows such as *The Antique Road Show* and *The Appraisal Fair* prove that virtually anything is collectible.

But, not all collectibles are a "portion" meant for financial stewardship. Some collections are just for fun and it is important that a potential collector know the difference.

I believe that the reason the Lord instructs us, through Solomon, to divide our assets into seven or eight portions is that not all individuals should have an eighth portion. I say this because collections are not usually liquid. They are slow to appreciate in value, they require highly specialized knowledge and they are subject to volatile increases and decreases in value. For these reasons if you intend to pursue a collection as an *investment portion*, it is important that you understand the following basic rules:

1. **First, you gotta have the love.** Collecting should spring from a passion within you for the item you are considering collecting. Appreciation for the beauty of a collection while it is under your stewardship should be your primary motivation to collect; a profit motive should be strictly a secondary concern.

2. **Gain knowledge.** Collections often require extensive knowledge that is gained over a long period of time. Collectibles are perhaps the most difficult group of assets to value and without a sound understanding of the collectible and the market for that collectible it is easy to overpay for your purchase. For example, stocks are traded over huge national exchanges, therefore you know the current value of a stock at the exact same time as any other potential buyer. However, if you walk into an antique store armed with a checkbook and very little knowledge, chances are you will pay dearly for your first lesson on the fair market value of a Chippendale chair.

3. **Be patient.** Collections are a labor of love and they tend to increase in value slowly. This is why you should collect only what you have a passion for and only after your financial house is in order.

4. **Protect your investment.** Collections often need special care and attention. Make sure that you do everything necessary to protect your collection from the ravages of time and store them in a safe and secure place.

And finally, remember this, Beanie Babies® are fun to collect if you are a child, but they are not an *investment* collectible or an eighth portion ... despite what the magazine says.

22

The Inheritance

The Living Bible

MAKE BELIEVE FOR A MOMENT. It's Saturday morning and your family has gone shopping. You decide to grab a mug of hot coffee and sit on the front porch in order to enjoy the splendor of a crisp autumn morning. The pale gray clouds resemble a large down blanket. Golden leaves dance and twirl up and down your street like little tornados. Occasionally the peaceful quiet is broken by a passing car and the distant voices of children at play. You stretch back, take a sip, and the coffee warms you.

Lost in thought, you don't even notice as a black limousine turns onto your street. But, now its peculiar behavior has caught your attention. It is slowly zig-zagging, pausing for a moment at each mailbox. The driver's dark tinted window rolls down and then up. This pattern continues as he proceeds from box to box. The car draws nearer and finally pulls up to your mailbox. It idles there for several minutes. You watch as the tinted window rolls down, but this time as it rolls back up the engine stops.

The rear door cracks open and a distinguished gentleman dressed in an expensive suit emerges. He walks over to your mailbox for a closer look, sees you sitting on the front porch and approaches. In one hand he is holding a leather briefcase and in the other a small package.

Stopping at the foot of your porch he asks if you're you, and when you acknowledge that you are, he smiles.

"Thank heaven I found you. I've been searching quite a while for you. My name is Samuels and I'm an attorney. I represent a distant relative of yours who has passed away and left you an inheritance."

An inheritance? For a moment you close your eyes and the word slips around your imagination like fine silk cloth. The pile of leaves in your front lawn is transformed into a pile of cash. Eyes open, you modestly reply, "How nice."

The stranger opens his briefcase and pulls out a few papers, "The procedure is really very simple, if you'll show me some identification and sign these papers, I'll conclude the transaction and be on my way."

Quickly you show him your driver's license and sign the necessary forms. And just as quickly, he hands you the package under his arm and walks away.

"That's it?"

"That's it."

"What is it?"

As the stranger opens his car door he turns your way one last time, "I have no idea. It came already wrapped with instructions to deliver it as I received it. I'm just the messenger. Have a good day, sir."

And there you sit, a cold cup of coffee in one hand, an odd gift in the other, watching as the stranger's tail lights disappear down the street.

Wandering back to your kitchen, you sit down and try to figure out what has just happened. Setting the package on the table, you take a closer look. It is a small box wrapped in plain brown paper. The only marking is your name scrawled across the front by an aging unsteady hand. The paper is held in place by yellowing string which breaks easily, exposing an old wooden box. Inside the box are two items, a letter and a book.

The letter is addressed to you. As you begin to read it you try to recall who the author was:

"You probably don't remember me, but I knew your father.

If you are reading this letter it means I have died and gone to heaven. My years on earth were good ones, I have no regrets. What I have learned is that the course of your life will be controlled by the decisions you make.

Decisions determine destiny.

Each day you make decisions regarding your family, your career, your relationships and your eternity. There will be times when the pain of the moment seems unbearable. There will be times when you feel as if you've been abandoned and left to wander aimlessly on a foreign field. During your days you will battle with the material, the physical and the spiritual. You will wrestle with anger and envy, lust and love, fear and foreboding, confusion and Christ. And while

*there may be times when each day appears to just random-
ly crash into the next one, I want you to know that there is
a plan and that your decisions will determine your destiny.*

*Which brings us to my gift for you. The enclosed book is very
special. It is a living Bible. The pages of this Bible contain
the answers to every decision common to man.*

This is your inheritance.

*To understand the gift, go alone into a quiet room and
search the scriptures.*

*A final word, do not be afraid of this gift ... be bold ... for
the Lord is with you."*

The letter is unsigned.

This is not the quiet morning you had planned. It's not even noon
and your day has been punctuated by a mysterious man, a bizarre letter, and an old Bible.

You sit there staring at the Bible lying on your kitchen table. You
can't help but admire this beautiful old book with the antique leather
binding and peeling gold letters revealing what is within ... The Holy
Bible. It feels good to the hand and smells remarkably new even
though its age is apparent. Gingerly picking it up, you allow the pages
to fall open.

And suddenly, it happens.

Before you can clearly see the title, Numbers, light explodes from
the pages.

The Bible drops from your hand and instantly what had been your
kitchen floor is now sand ... night surrounds you ... you jump up to
run, but there is no place to go. Where a moment ago there were

kitchen cabinets, now there is a campfire surrounded by men arguing violently.

Frozen by the transformation, all you can do is stand and listen.

One of the men dressed in ancient clothing yells at the others, "We do have a choice! We can take the land that God has promised to us, or we can ignore God, turn our back on his gift and die like cowards in this forsaken desert. As for me and my family we choose to believe God and to receive the gift He has promised us."

But he is shouted down by the others, "No, we can't. We can't. We are like grasshoppers. If we leave this desert we will surely die. We'd have been better off if we had stayed in Egypt."

The shouting continues until two of the men stalk off in utter disgust, leaving a nation to cower around a campfire.

It is then that you notice the Bible you dropped lying in the sand at your feet. You reach down to retrieve it and as your hand touches the binding, you are back in the kitchen once again.

Bolting from your chair, you grab the letter that came with the gift and reread it.

"... The enclosed book is very special. It is a living Bible ..."

Still shaking, you put the book down on the kitchen table and back away, but something draws you to it. Placing both hands on its cover a strange peace fills you and from somewhere within you find the courage to open it. Once again, a flash of light transforms your kitchen, this time into the loft of an ancient home.

The room is dark, lit only by a solitary candle burning next to a small wooden bed. A man kneels at the side of the bed weeping uncontrollably. His tears fall on a young girl lying motionless in the bed. His shoulders are wrapped in a tallith, a special prayer shawl indicating that this man is an important leader in the synagogue. His heart is pierced with pain as he watches his beloved child drift from life to death.

His wife enters the room and kneels next to him softly taking his hand, "There is a healer in town. They say he works great miracles, that he has the gift of healing. We must ask him to come and heal our daughter."

Her husband's shoulders slump forward burying his face in his hands. "I know, I've heard, but they say he's a blasphemer and that his beliefs are not ours. The people of the synagogue look to me for leadership. What will they say if we invite him here?"

"I don't know what they will say, but I do know that if we choose not to seek the healer, she will die."

The man looks at his priestly robes and then at his lifeless daughter. "I'll go and talk to the healer."

Closing your Bible, you're back in the kitchen, exhausted.

And so the day goes. One moment you are standing in your home and the next moment you are standing ankle deep in a river watching Gideon whittle his army down to three hundred men. Common sense tells Gideon that he needs more men. God tells him to obey. The choice is his. Turning the page you watch as his tiny army routes one hundred and thirty-five thousand Midianites and the Israelites reclaim their inheritance.

One moment in your kitchen drinking coffee, the next in Solomon's palace drinking in the wisdom of the ages.

One more time you open the gift and this time a skull-shaped rock dominates the landscape in front of you. You know where you are, Golgotha. You know what you'll find as you ascend to the top of the hill, three crosses holding three dead men. What you didn't expect to find at the top of the hill was a lone Roman soldier. His arms are wrapped around the center cross, his head resting on the feet of Christ, his eyes filled with tears, his face torn with remorse. As you move closer you hear him repeating over and over again, "Forgive me, forgive me, forgive me, surely you were the son of God. From this day forward I will follow you." And having made his choice, he lays down his sword and shield and walks away.

Closing your Bible once again, you return home.

* * * * * * * * * *

Here's the thing.

It's not make believe.

Ancient hands have crafted a love letter to each of us. Every page is a guidepost staked in place by the Creator. Each chapter and verse become a divine beacon lighting an eternal path home as it directs our steps through the desert to the cross.

We have been given the inheritance ... The Bible, God's truth alive today demonstrating His wisdom, His power, and His unending love for us.

My hope is that this book offers some information and guidance for your personal finances, but that

"your faith might not rest on men's wisdom,
but on God's power."
(1 Corinthians 2:5)

Epilogue

Do You Know Jesus?

MY HEARTFELT DESIRE is that this book has moved you toward a closer relationship with the Lord. If you do not know Jesus as your personal Lord and Savior, please pray this prayer:

Lord Jesus, I am a sinner in need of a Savior. I believe that You are the Son of God and that you died on the cross, a living sacrifice for my sins. I surrender my life to You. Please forgive me for my sins and create in me a new heart that desires to serve You all the days of my life. I accept You as my Lord and Savior.
Amen.

You may contact Robert Katz at:

Katz & Asher, Ltd.
1515 Poydras Street, Suite 1800
New Orleans, Louisiana. 70112
504-525-8524
rwkatz@katzasher.com